Patience by Gilbert & Sullivan

or BUNTHORNE'S BRIDE

Libretto by William S. Gilbert
Music by Arthur Sullivan

The partnership between William Schwenck Gilbert and Arthur Seymour Sullivan and their canon of Savoy Operas is rightly lauded by all lovers of comic opera the world over.

Gilbert's sharp, funny words and Sullivan's deliciously lively and hummable tunes create a world that is distinctly British in view but has the world as its audience.

Both men were exceptionally talented and gifted in their own right and wrote much, often with other partners, that still stands the test of time. However, together as a team they created Light or Comic Operas of a standard that have had no rivals equal to their standard, before or since. That's quite an achievement.

To be recognised by the critics is one thing but their commercial success was incredible. The profits were astronomical, allowing for the building of their own purpose built theatre – The Savoy Theatre.

Beginning with the first of their fourteen collaborations, Thespis in 1871 and travelling through many classics including The Sorcerer (1877), H.M.S. Pinafore (1878), The Pirates of Penzance (1879), The Mikado (1885), The Gondoliers (1889) to their finale in 1896 with The Grand Duke, Gilbert & Sullivan created a legacy that is constantly revived and admired in theatres and other media to this very day.

Index of Contents

Patience or Bunthorne's Bride was the sixth opera by Gilbert & Sullivan. It debuted on April 23, 1881 at the Opera Comique before transferring to the new Savoy Theatre on October 10, 1881. It ran for a total of 578 performances.

DRAMATIS PERSONAE
Officers of Dragoon Guards
COLONEL CALVERLEY, Baritone

MAJOR MURGATROYD, Baritone
LIEUTENANT THE DUKE OF DUNSTABLE, Tenor
REGINALD BUNTHORNE (A Fleshly Poet) Light Baritone

ARCHIBALD GROSVENOR (An Idyllic Poet), Baritone

MR. BUNTHORNE'S SOLICITOR, Non-singing

Rapturous Maidens
THE LADY ANGELA, Mezzo-Soprano
THE LADY SAPHIR, Mezzo-Soprano
THE LADY ELLA, Soprano
THE LADY JANE, Contralto

PATIENCE (A Dairy Maid), Soprano

CHORUS of Rapturous MAIDENS and Officers of DRAGOON GUARDS

SCENES
ACT I—Exterior of Castle Bunthorne
ACT II—A Glade

MUSICAL NUMBERS

Overture
ACT I
1 - Twenty love-sick maidens we (Opening Chorus and Solos) – Maidens, Angela and Ella
2 - Still brooding on their mad infatuation (Recitative) – Patience, Saphir, Angela, and Chorus
   I cannot tell what this love may be (Solo) – Patience
2a - Twenty love-sick maidens we (Chorus) – Maidens
3 - The soldiers of our Queen (Chorus and Solo) – Dragoons and Colonel
4 - In a doleful train (Chorus and Solos) – Maidens, Ella, Angela, Saphir, Dragoons, and Bunthorne
4a - Twenty love-sick maidens we (Chorus) – Maidens
5 - When I first put this uniform on (Solo and Chorus) – Colonel and Dragoons
6 - Am I alone and unobserved? (Recitative and Solo) – Bunthorne
7 - Long years ago, fourteen maybe (Duet) – Patience and Angela
8 - Prithee, pretty maiden (Duet) – Patience and Grosvenor
8a - Though to marry you would very selfish be (Duet) – Patience and Grosvenor
9 - Let the merry cymbals sound (Finale of Act I) – Ensemble
ACT II
10 - In such eyes as maidens cherish (Opening Chorus) – Maidens
11 - Sad is that woman's lot (Recitative and Solo) – Jane
12 - Turn, oh, turn in this direction (Chorus) – Maidens
13 - A magnet hung in a hardware shop (Solo and Chorus) – Grosvenor and Maidens

ACT I

[Scene: Exterior of Castle Bunthorne, the gateway to which is seen, R.U.E., and is approached by a drawbridge over a moat. A rocky eminence R. with steps down to the stage. In front of it, a rustic bench, on which ANGELA is seated, with ELLA on her left. Young Ladies wearing aesthetic draperies are grouped about the stage from R. to L.C., SAPHIR being near the L. end of the group. The Ladies play on lutes, etc., as they sing, and all are in the last stage of despair.]

No. 1. Twenty love-sick maidens we
(Opening Chorus and Solos) Maidens, Angela, and Ella

MAIDENS
Twenty love-sick maidens we,
Love-sick all against our will.
Twenty years hence we shall be
Twenty love-sick maidens still!
Twenty love-sick maidens we,
And we die for love of thee!
Twenty love-sick maidens we,
Love-sick all against our will.
Twenty years hence we shall be
Twenty love-sick maidens still!

ANGELA
Love feeds on hope, they say, or love will die;

MAIDENS
Ah, miserie!

ANGELA
Yet my love lives, although no hope have I!

MAIDENS
Ah, miserie!

ANGELA
Alas, poor heart, go hide thyself away,
To weeping concords tune thy roundelay!

Ah, miserie!

MAIDENS
All our love is all for one,
Yet that love he heedeth not,
He is coy and cares for none,
Sad and sorry is our lot!
Ah, miserie!

ELLA
Go, breaking heart,
Go, dream of love requited!
Go, foolish heart,
Go, dream of lovers plighted;
Go, madcap heart,
Go, dream of never waking;
And in thy dream
Forget that thou art breaking!

MAIDENS
Ah, miserie!

ELLA
Forget that thou art breaking!

MAIDENS
Twenty love-sick maidens we,
Love-sick all against our will.
Twenty years hence we shall be
Twenty love-sick maidens still.
Ah, miserie!

ANGELA
There is a strange magic in this love of ours! Rivals as we all are in the affections of our Reginald, the very hopelessness of our love is a bond that binds us to one another!

SAPHIR
Jealousy is merged in misery. While he, the very cynosure of our eyes and hearts, remains icy insensible — what have we to strive for?

ELLA
The love of maidens is, to him, as interesting as the taxes!

SAPHIR
Would that it were! He pays his taxes.

ANGELA
And cherishes the receipts!

[Enter LADY JANE, L.U.E.]

SAPHIR
Happy receipts!

[All sigh heavily]

JANE [L.C., suddenly]
Fools!

[They start, and turn to her]

ANGELA
I beg your pardon?

JANE
Fools and blind! The man loves — wildly loves!

ANGELA
But whom? None of us!

JANE
No, none of us. His weird fancy has lighted, for the nonce, on Patience, the village milkmaid!

SAPHIR
On Patience? Oh, it cannot be!

JANE
Bah! But yesterday I caught him in her dairy, eating fresh butter with a tablespoon. Today he is not well!

SAPHIR
But Patience boasts that she has never loved — that love is, to her, a sealed book! Oh, he cannot be serious!

JANE
`Tis but a fleeting fancy — `twill quickly wear away.
[aside, coming down-stage]
Oh, Reginald, if you but knew what a wealth of golden love is waiting for you, stored up in this rugged old bosom of mine, the milkmaid's triumph would be short indeed!

[PATIENCE appears on an eminence, R. She looks down with pity on the despondent Ladies.]

No. 2. Still brooding on their mad infatuation!
(Recitative) Patience, Saphir, Angela, and Maidens

PATIENCE

Still brooding on their mad infatuation!
I thank thee, Love, thou comest not to me!
Far happier I, free from thy ministration,
Than dukes or duchesses who love can be!

SAPHIR [looking up]
`Tis Patience — happy girl! Loved by a poet!

PATIENCE
Your pardon, ladies. I intrude upon you! [Going]

ANGELA
Nay, pretty child, come hither. [PATIENCE descends.] Is it true that you have never loved?

PATIENCE
Most true indeed.

SOPRANOS
Most marvelous!

ALTOS
And most deplorable!
I cannot tell what this love may be
(Solo)
Patience

PATIENCE
I cannot tell what this love may be
[L.C.]
That cometh to all but not to me.
It cannot be kind as they'd imply,
Or why do these ladies sigh?

It cannot be joy and rapture deep,
Or why do these gentle ladies weep?
It cannot be blissful as `tis said,
Or why are their eyes so wondrous red?

Though ev'rywhere true love I see
A-coming to all, but not to me,
I cannot tell what this love may be!
For I am blithe and I am gay,
While they sit sighing night and day.

PATIENCE	**ALL**
For I am blithe and I am gay,	Yes, she is blithe and she is gay,
Think of the gulf `twixt them and me	Yes, she is blithe and she is gay,
Think of the gulf `twixt them, and me	Yes, she is blithe and she is gay,

Fal la la la la la la la la la la la la la la la   La la la la la la la la la la la la,
And miserie!   Ah, miserie!

[She dances across R. and back to R.C.]

PATIENCE
If love is a thorn, they show no wit
Who foolishly hug and foster it.
If love is a weed, how simple they
Who gather it, day by day!

If love is a nettle that makes you smart,
Then why do you wear it next your heart?
And if it be none of these, say I,
Ah, why do you sit and sob and sigh?

Though ev'rywhere true love I see
A-coming to all, but not to me,
I cannot tell what this love may be!
For I am blithe and I am gay,
While they sit sighing night and day.

PATIENCE	**ALL**
For I am blithe and I am gay,	Yes, she is blithe and she is gay,
Think of the gulf 'twixt them and me,	Yes, she is blithe and she is gay,
Think of the gulf 'twixt them and me,	Yes, she is blithe and she is gay,
Fal la la la la la la la la la la la la la la	La la la la la la la la la la la,
And miserie!	Ah, miserie!

ANGELA
Ah, Patience, if you have never loved, you have never known true happiness!

[All sigh.]

PATIENCE [C.]
But the truly happy always seem to have so much on their minds. The truly happy never seem quite well.

JANE [coming L.C.]
There is a transcendentality of delirium — an acute accentuation of supremest ecstasy — which the earthy might easily mistake for indigestion. But it is not indigestion — it is aesthetic transfiguration! [to the others.] Enough of babble. Come!

PATIENCE [stopping her as she turns to go up C.]
But stay, I have some news for you. The 35th Dragoon Guards have halted in the village, and are even now on their way to this very spot.

ANGELA

The 35th Dragoon Guards!

SAPHIR
They are fleshly men, of full habit!

ELLA
We care nothing for Dragoon Guards!

PATIENCE
But, bless me, you were all engaged to them a year ago!

SAPHIR
A year ago!

ANGELA
My poor child, you don't understand these things. A year ago they were very well in our eyes, but since then our tastes have been etherealized, our perceptions exalted. [To the others] Come, it is time to lift up our voices in morning carol to our Reginald. Let us to his door!

[ANGELA leading, the LADIES go off, two and two, JANE last, over the drawbridge into the castle, singing refrain of "Twenty love-sick maidens", and, as before, accompanying themselves on harps, etc.]

No. 2a. Twenty love-sick maidens we
(Chorus) Maidens

MAIDENS
Twenty love-sick maidens we,
Love-sick all against our will.
Twenty years hence we shall be
Twenty love-sick maidens still!
Ah, miserie!

[PATIENCE watches them in surprise, and, with a gesture of complete bafflement, climbs the rock and goes off the way she entered.]

[The officers of the DRAGOON GUARDS enter, R., led by the MAJOR. They form their line across the front of the stage.]

No. 3. The soldiers of our Queen
(Chorus and Solo) Dragoons and Colonel

DRAGOONS
The soldiers of our Queen
Are linked in friendly tether;
Upon the battle scene
They fight the foe together.

There ev'ry mother's son

Prepared to fight and fall is;
The enemy of one
The enemy of all is!
The enemy of one
The enemy of all is!

[On an order from the MAJOR they fall back.]

[Enter the COLONEL. ALL salute.]

COLONEL
If you want a receipt for that popular mystery,
Known to the world as a Heavy Dragoon,

DRAGOONS [saluting]
Yes, yes, yes, yes, yes, yes, yes!

COLONEL
Take all the remarkable people in history,
Rattle them off to a popular tune.

DRAGOONS
Yes, yes, yes, yes, yes, yes, yes!

COLONEL
The pluck of Lord Nelson on board of the Victory—
Genius of Bismarck devising a plan—
The humour of Fielding (which sounds contradictory)—
Coolness of Paget about to trepan—
The science of Jullien, the eminent musico—
Wit of Macaulay, who wrote of Queen Anne—
The pathos of Paddy, as rendered by Boucicault—
Style of the Bishop of Sodor and Man—
The dash of a D'Orsay, divested of quackery—
Narrative powers of Dickens and Thackeray—
Victor Emmanuel — peak-haunting Peveril—
Thomas Aquinas, and Doctor Sacheverell—
Tupper and Tennyson — Daniel Defoe—
Anthony Trollope and Mister Guizot! Ah!

DRAGOONS
Yes, yes, yes, yes, yes, yes, yes!

COLONEL	**DRAGOONS**
Take of these elements all	A Heavy Dragoon,
that is fusible	a Heavy Dragoon,
Melt them all down in a	A Heavy Dragoon,
pipkin or crucible—	a Heavy Dragoon,

Set them to simmer,
and take off the scum,
And a Heavy Dragoon
is the residuum!

A Heavy Dragoon,
a Heavy Dragoon,
Is the residuum!

COLONEL
If you want a receipt for this soldier-like paragon,
Get at the wealth of the Czar (if you can)—
The family pride of a Spaniard from Aragon—
Force of Mephisto pronouncing a ban—
A smack of Lord Waterford, reckless and rollicky—
Swagger of Roderick, heading his clan—
The keen penetration of Paddington Pollaky—
Grace of an Odalisque on a divan—
The genius strategic of Caesar or Hannibal—
Skill of Sir Garnet in thrashing a cannibal—
Flavour of Hamlet — the Stranger, a touch of him—
Little of Manfred (but not very much of him)—
Beadle of Burlington — Richardson's show—
Mister Micawber and Madame Tussaud! Ah!

DRAGOONS
Yes, yes, yes, yes, yes, yes, yes!

COLONEL	**DRAGOONS**
Take of these elements all	A Heavy Dragoon,
that is fusible	a Heavy Dragoon,
Melt them all down in a	A Heavy Dragoon,
pipkin or crucible—	a Heavy Dragoon,
Set them to simmer,	A Heavy Dragoon,
and take off the scum,	a Heavy Dragoon,
And a Heavy Dragoon	Is the residuum!
is the residuum!	

COLONEL
Well, here we are once more on the scene of our former triumphs. But where's the Duke?

[Enter DUKE, listlessly, and in low spirits.]

DUKE
Here I am!

[Sighs.]

COLONEL
Come, cheer up, don't give way!

DUKE

Oh, for that, I'm as cheerful as a poor devil can be expected to be who has the misfortune to be a Duke, with a thousand a day!

MAJOR
Humph! Most men would envy you!

DUKE
Envy me? Tell me, Major, are you fond of toffee?

MAJOR
Very!

COLONEL
We are all fond of toffee.

ALL
We are!

DUKE
Yes, and toffee in moderation is a capital thing. But to live on toffee — toffee for breakfast, toffee for dinner, toffee for tea — to have it supposed that you care for nothing but toffee, and that you would consider yourself insulted if anything but toffee were offered to you — how would you like that?

COLONEL
I can quite believe that, under those circumstances, even toffee would become monotonous.

DUKE
For "toffee" read flattery, adulation, and abject deference, carried to such a pitch that I began, at last, to think that man was born bent at an angle of forty-five degrees! Great heavens, what is there to adulate in me? Am I particularly intelligent, or remarkably studious, or excruciatingly witty, or unusually accomplished, or exceptionally virtuous?

COLONEL
You're about as commonplace a young man as ever I saw.

ALL
You are!

DUKE
Exactly! That's it exactly! That describes me to a T! Thank you all very much!

[Shakes hands with the COLONEL]

Well, I couldn't stand it any longer, so I joined this second-class cavalry regiment. In the army, thought I, I shall be occasionally snubbed, perhaps even bullied, who knows? The thought was rapture, and here I am.

COLONEL [looking off]

Yes, and here are the ladies!

DUKE
But who is the gentleman with the long hair?

COLONEL
I don't know.

DUKE
He seems popular!

COLONEL
He does seem popular!

[The DRAGOONS back up R., watching the entrance of the Ladies. BUNTHORNE enters, L.U.E., followed by the LADIES, two and two, playing on harps as before. He is composing a poem, and is quite absorbed. He sees no one, but walks across the stage, followed by the LADIES, who take no notice of the DRAGOONS — to the surprise and indignation of those officers.]

[BUNTHORNE, the LADIES following, comes slowly down L. and then crosses the stage to R.]

No. 4. In a doleful train
(Chorus and Solos) Maidens, Ella, Angela, Saphir, Dragoons, and Bunthorne

MAIDENS
In a doleful train
Two and two we walk all day—
For we love in vain!
None so sorrowful as they
Who can only sigh and say,
Woe is me, alackaday!
Woe is me, alackaday!

DRAGOONS
Now is not this ridiculous, and is not this preposterous?
A thorough-paced absurdity — explain it if you can.
Instead of rushing eagerly to cherish us and foster us,
They all prefer this melancholy literary man.
Instead of slyly peering at us,
Casting looks endearing at us,
Blushing at us, flushing at us, flirting with a fan;
They're actually sneering at us, fleering at us, jeering at us!
Pretty sort of treatment for a military man!
They're actually sneering at us, fleering at us, jeering at us!
Pretty sort of treatment for a military man!

[BUNTHORNE, C.]

ANGELA [R. of BUNTHORNE]
Mystic poet, hear our prayer,
Twenty love-sick maidens we—
Young and wealthy, dark and fair,
All of county family.
And we die for love of thee—
Twenty love-sick maidens we!

MAIDENS
Yes, we die for love of thee—
Twenty love-sick maidens we!

BUNTHORNE [crossing to L.]
Though my book I seem to scan
In a rapt ecstatic way,
Like a literary man
Who despises female clay,
I hear plainly all they say,
Twenty love-sick maidens they!

[BUNTHORNE crosses to C.]

DRAGOONS [to each other]
He hears plainly all they say,
Twenty love-sick maidens they!

SAPHIR [L. of BUNTHORNE]
Though so excellently wise,
For a moment mortal be,
Deign to raise thy purple eyes
From thy heart-drawn poesy.
Twenty lovesick maidens see—
Each is kneeling on her knee!

[All kneel.]

MAIDENS
Twenty love-sick maidens see—
Each is kneeling on her knee!

BUNTHORNE [going R.]
Though, as I remarked before,
Any one convinced would be
That some transcendental lore
Is monopolizing me,
Round the corner I can see
Each is kneeling on her knee!

DRAGOONS
Round the corner he can see
Each is kneeling on her knee!

Now is not this ridiculous, and is not this preposterous?
A thorough-paced absurdity — ridiculous! Preposterous!
Explain it if you can.

MAIDENS	DRAGOONS
In a doleful train	Now is not this ridiculous, and is not this preposterous?
Two and two we walk all day,	A thorough-paced absurdity—explain it if you can
None so sorrowful as they	They all prefer this melancholy literary man.
Who can	Instead of slyly peering at us,
only	Casting looks endearing at us
sigh and say	Blushing at us, flushing at us, flirting with a fan;
Woe is me,	They're actually sneering at us, fleering at us, jeering at us!
Alack-a-day!	Pretty sort of treatment for a military man!
Twenty love-sick maidens we,	Now is not this ridiculous, and is not this preposterous?
And we	They all prefer this melancholy literary man.
die for love of	Now is not this ridiculous, and is not this preposterous?
Thee!	They all prefer this melancholy,
Yes, we die	melancholy literary man
for love of thee!	Now is not this ridiculous, and is not this preposterous?

COLONEL [R.C.]
Angela! what is the meaning of this?

ANGELA [C.]
Oh, sir, leave us; our minds are but ill-tuned to light love-talk.

MAJOR [L.C.]
But what in the world has come over you all?

JANE [L.C.]
Bunthorne! He has come over us. He has come among us, and he has idealized us.

DUKE
Has he succeeded in idealizing you?

JANE
He has!

DUKE
Good old Bunthorne!

JANE
My eyes are open; I droop despairingly; I am soulfully intense; I am limp and I cling!

[During this BUNTHORNE is seen in all the agonies of composition. The LADIES are watching him intently as he writhes. At last he hits on the word he wants and writes it down. A general sense of relief.]

BUNTHORNE
Finished! At last! Finished!

[He staggers, overcome with the mental strain, into the arms of the COLONEL.]

COLONEL
Are you better now?

BUNTHORNE
Yes — oh, it's you! — I am better now. The poem is finished, and my soul has gone out into it. That was all. It was nothing worth mentioning, it occurs three times a day.

[Sees PATIENCE, who has entered during this scene.]

Ah, Patience! Dear Patience!

[Holds her hand; she seems frightened.]

ANGELA
Will it please you read it to us, sir?

SAPHIR
This we supplicate.

[All kneel.]

BUNTHORNE
Shall I?

DRAGOONS
No!

BUNTHORNE [annoyed — to PATIENCE]
I will read it if you bid me!

PATIENCE [much frightened]
You can if you like!

BUNTHORNE
It is a wild, weird, fleshy thing; yet very tender, very yearning, very precious. It is called, "Oh, Hollow! Hollow! Hollow!"

PATIENCE
Is it a hunting song?

BUNTHORNE
A hunting song? No, it is not a hunting song. It is the wail of the poet's heart on discovering that everything is commonplace. To understand it, cling passionately to one another and think of faint lilies.

[They do so as he recites]

"OH, HOLLOW! HOLLOW! HOLLOW!"

What time the poet hath hymned
The writhing maid, lithe-limbed,
Quivering on amaranthine asphodel,
How can he paint her woes,
Knowing, as well he knows,
That all can be set right with calomel?

When from the poet's plinth
The amorous colocynth
Yearns for the aloe, faint with rapturous thrills,
How can he hymn their throes
Knowing, as well he knows,
That they are only uncompounded pills?

Is it, and can it be,
Nature hath this decree,
Nothing poetic in the world shall dwell?
Or that in all her works
Something poetic lurks,
Even in colocynth and calomel?
I cannot tell.

[He goes off, L.U.E. ALL turn and watch him, not speaking until he has gone.]

ANGELA
How purely fragrant!

SAPHIR
How earnestly precious!

PATIENCE
Well, it seems to me to be nonsense.

SAPHIR
Nonsense, yes, perhaps — but oh, what precious nonsense!

COLONEL
This is all very well, but you seem to forget that you are engaged to us.

SAPHIR

It can never be. You are not Empyrean. You are not Della Cruscan. You are not even Early English. Oh, be Early English ere it is too late!

[OFFICERS look at each other in astonishment.]

JANE [looking at uniform]
Red and Yellow! Primary colors! Oh, South Kensington!

DUKE
We didn't design our uniforms, but we don't see how they could be improved!

JANE
No, you wouldn't. Still, there is a cobwebby grey velvet, with a tender bloom like cold gravy, which, made Florentine fourteenth century, trimmed with Venetian leather and Spanish altar lace, and surmounted with something Japanese — it matters not what — would at least be Early English! Come, maidens.

[Exeunt MAIDENS, L.U.E., two and two, singing refrain of "Twenty love-sick maidens we". PATIENCE goes off L. The OFFICERS watch the LADIES go off in astonishment.]

No. 4a. Twenty love-sick maidens we
(Chorus) Maidens

[As the MAIDENS depart, the DRAGOONS spread across the stage.]

MAIDENS
Twenty love-sick maidens we,
Love-sick all against our will.
Twenty years hence we shall be
Twenty love-sick maidens still!
Ah, miserie!

DUKE
Gentlemen, this is an insult to the British uniform.

COLONEL
A uniform that has been as successful in the courts of Venus as on the field of Mars!

No. 5. When I first put this uniform on
(Solo and Chorus) Colonel and Dragoons

[The DRAGOONS form their original line.]

Song—**COLONEL**
When I first put this uniform on,
I said, as I looked in the glass,
"It's one to a million
That any civilian

My figure and form will surpass.
Gold lace has a charm for the fair,
And I've plenty of that, and to spare,
While a lover's professions,
When uttered in Hessians,
Are eloquent ev'rywhere!"
A fact that I counted upon,
When I first put this uniform on!

CHORUS of DRAGOONS
By a simple coincidence, few
Could ever have counted upon,
The same thing occurred to me,
When I first put this uniform on!

COLONEL
I said, when I first put it on,
"It is plain to the veriest dunce,
That every beauty
Will feel it her duty
To yield to its glamour at once.
They will see that I'm freely gold-laced
In a uniform handsome and chaste"—
But the peripatetics
Of long-haired aesthetics
Are very much more to their taste—
Which I never counted upon,
When I first put this uniform on!

CHORUS
By a simple coincidence, few
Could ever have reckoned upon,
I didn't anticipate that,
When I first put this uniform on!

[The DRAGOONS go off angrily, R.]

[Enter BUNTHORNE, L.U.E., who changes his manner and becomes intensely melodramatic.]

No. 6. Am I alone and unobserved?
(Recitative and Solo) Bunthorne

BUNTHORNE [Up-stage, he looks off L. and R.]
Am I alone,
And unobserved? I am!
[comes down]
Then let me own
I'm an aesthetic sham!

[and walks tragically to down-stage, C.]

This air severe
Is but a mere
Veneer!

This cynic smile
Is but a wile
Of guile!

This costume chaste
Is but good taste
Misplaced!

Let me confess!
A languid love for Lilies does not blight me!
Lank limbs and haggard cheeks do not delight me!
I do not care for dirty greens
By any means.
I do not long for all one sees
That's Japanese.
I am not fond of uttering platitudes
In stained-glass attitudes.
In short, my mediaevalism's affectation,
Born of a morbid love of admiration!

[Tiptoes up-stage, looking L. and R., and comes back down, C.]

If you're anxious for to shine in the high aesthetic line as a man of culture rare,
You must get up all the germs of the transcendental terms, and plant them ev'rywhere.
You must lie upon the daisies and discourse in novel phrases of your complicated state of mind,
The meaning doesn't matter if it's only idle chatter of a transcendental kind.

And ev'ry one will say,
As you walk your mystic way,
"If this young man expresses himself in terms too deep for me,
Why, what a very singularly deep young man this deep young man must be!"

Be eloquent in praise of the very dull old days which have long since passed away,
And convince 'em, if you can, that the reign of good Queen Anne was Culture's palmiest day.
Of course you will pooh-pooh whatever's fresh and new, and declare it's crude and mean,
For Art stopped short in the cultivated court of the Empress Josephine.

And ev'ryone will say,
As you walk your mystic way,
"If that's not good enough for him which is good enough for me,
Why, what a very cultivated kind of youth this kind of youth must be!"

Then a sentimental passion of a vegetable fashion must excite your languid spleen,
An attachment a la Plato for a bashful young potato, or a not-too-French French bean!
Though the Philistines may jostle, you will rank as an apostle in the high aesthetic band,
If you walk down Piccadilly with a poppy or a lily in your medieval hand.

And ev'ryone will say,
As you walk your flow'ry way,
"If he's content with a vegetable love which would certainly not suit me,
Why, what a most particularly pure young man this pure young man must be!"

[At the end of his song, PATIENCE enters, L. He sees her.]

BUNTHORNE
Ah! Patience, come hither. [She comes to him timidly.] I am pleased with thee. The bitter-hearted one, who finds all else hollow, is pleased with thee. For you are not hollow. Are you?

PATIENCE
No, thanks, I have dined; but — I beg your pardon — I interrupt you.

[Turns to go; he stops her.]

BUNTHORNE
Life is made up of interruptions. The tortured soul, yearning for solitude, writhes under them. Oh, but my heart is a-weary! Oh, I am a cursed thing! [She attempts to escape.] Don't go.

PATIENCE
Really, I'm very sorry.

BUNTHORNE
Tell me, girl, do you ever yearn?

PATIENCE
I earn my living.

BUNTHORNE [impatiently]
No, no! Do you know what it is to be heart-hungry? Do you know what it is to yearn for the Indefinable, and yet to be brought face to face, dally, with the Multiplication Table? Do you know what it is to seek oceans and to find puddles? That's my case. Oh, I am a cursed thing! [She turns again.] Don't go.

PATIENCE
If you please, I don't understand you — you frighten me!

BUNTHORNE
Don't be frightened — it's only poetry.

PATIENCE
Well, if that's poetry, I don't like poetry.

BUNTHORNE [eagerly]

Don't you? [aside] Can I trust her? [aloud] Patience, you don't like poetry — well, between you and me, I don't like poetry. It's hollow, unsubstantial — unsatisfactory. What's the use of yearning for Elysian Fields when you know you can't get `em, and would only let `em out on building leases if you had `em?

PATIENCE

Sir, I—

BUNTHORNE

Patience, I have long loved you. Let me tell you a secret. I am not as bilious as I look. If you like, I will cut my hair. There is more innocent fun within me than a casual spectator would imagine. You have never seen me frolicsome. Be a good girl — a very good girl — and one day you shall. If you are fond of touch-and-go jocularity — this is the shop for it.

PATIENCE

Sir, I will speak plainly. In the matter of love I am untaught. I have never loved but my great-aunt. But I am quite certain that, under any circumstances, I couldn't possibly love you.

BUNTHORNE

Oh, you think not?

PATIENCE

I'm quite sure of it. Quite sure. Quite.

BUNTHORNE

Very good. Life is henceforth a blank. I don't care what becomes of me. I have only to ask that you will not abuse my confidence; though you despise me, I am extremely popular with the other young ladies.

PATIENCE

I only ask that you will leave me and never renew the subject.

BUNTHORNE

Certainly. Broken-hearted and desolate, I go.

[Goes up-stage, suddenly turns and recites.]

"Oh, to be wafted away,
From this black Aceldama of sorrow,
Where the dust of an earthy to-day
Is the earth of a dusty to-morrow!"

It is a little thing of my own. I call it "Heart Foam". I shall not publish it. Farewell! Patience, Patience, farewell!

[Exit BUNTHORNE.]

PATIENCE

What on earth does it all mean? Why does he love me?

Why does he expect me to love him? [going R.] He's not a relation! It frightens me!

[Enter ANGELA, L.]

ANGELA
Why, Patience, what is the matter?

PATIENCE
Lady Angela, tell me two things. Firstly, what on earth is this love that upsets everybody; and, secondly, how is it to be distinguished from insanity?

ANGELA
Poor blind child! Oh, forgive her, Eros! Why, love is of all passions the most essential! It is the embodiment of purity, the abstraction of refinement! It is the one unselfish emotion in this whirlpool of grasping greed!

PATIENCE
Oh, dear, oh! [beginning to cry]

ANGELA
Why are you crying?

PATIENCE
To think that I have lived all these years without having experienced this ennobling and unselfish passion! Why, what a wicked girl I must be! For it is unselfish, isn't it?

ANGELA
Absolutely! Love that is tainted with selfishness is no love. Oh, try, try, try to love! It really isn't difficult if you give your whole mind to it.

PATIENCE
I'll set about it at once. I won't go to bed until I'm head over ears in love with somebody.

ANGELA
Noble girl! But is it possible that you have never loved anybody?

PATIENCE
Yes, one.

ANGELA
Ah! Whom?

PATIENCE
My great-aunt—

ANGELA
Great-aunts don't count.

PATIENCE

Then there's nobody. At least — no, nobody. Not since I was a baby. But that doesn't count, I suppose.

ANGELA

I don't know. Tell me about it.

No. 7. Long years ago, fourteen maybe
(Duet) Patience and Angela

PATIENCE [R.]

Long years ago — fourteen, maybe,
When but a tiny babe of four,
Another baby played with me,
My elder by a year or more;

A little child of beauty rare,
With marv'lous eyes and wondrous hair,
Who, in my child-eyes, seemed to me
All that a little child should be!

[She goes to ANGELA, L.C.]

Ah, how we loved, that child and I!
How pure our baby joy!
How true our love — and, by the bye,
He was a little boy!

ANGELA

Ah, old, old tale of Cupid's touch!
I thought as much — I thought as much!
He was a little boy!

PATIENCE

Pray don't misconstrue what I say—
Remember, pray — remember, pray,
He was a little boy!

ANGELA

No doubt! Yet, spite of all your pains,
The interesting fact remains -
He was a little boy!

BOTH

Ah, yes, in/No doubt, yet spite of all my/your pains,
The interesting fact remains—
He was a little boy!
He was a little boy!

[Exit ANGELA, L.]

PATIENCE [R.C.]

It's perfectly dreadful to think of the appalling state I must be in! I had no idea that love was a duty. No wonder they all look so unhappy! Upon my word, I hardly like to associate with myself. I don't think I'm respectable. I'll go at once and fall in love with... [As she turns to go up R., GROSVENOR enters, R.U.E. She sees him and turns back.] a stranger!

No. 8. Prithee, pretty maiden
(Duet) Patience and Grosvenor

GROSVENOR [up-stage, R.]

Prithee, pretty maiden — prithee, tell me true,
(Hey, but I'm doleful, willow willow waly!)
Have you e'er a lover a-dangling after you?
Hey willow waly O!
[coming down-stage]

I would fain discover
If you have a lover!
Hey willow waly O!

PATIENCE [L.]

Gentle sir, my heart is frolicsome and free—
(Hey, but he's doleful, willow willow waly!)
Nobody I care for comes a-courting me—
Hey willow waly O!
Nobody I care for
Comes a-courting — therefore,
Hey willow waly O!

GROSVENOR [C.]

Prithee, pretty maiden, will you marry me?
(Hey, but I'm hopeful, willow willow waly!)
I may say, at once, I'm a man of propertee—
Hey willow waly O!
Money, I despise it;
Many people prize it,
Hey willow waly O!

PATIENCE

Gentle Sir, although to marry I design—
(Hey, but he's hopeful, willow willow waly!)
As yet I do not know you, and so I must decline.
Hey willow waly O!
To other maidens go you—
As yet I do not know you,

BOTH
Hey willow waly O!

GROSVENOR
Patience! Can it be that you don't recognize me?

PATIENCE [down L.]
Recognize you? No, indeed I don't!

GROSVENOR
Have fifteen years so greatly changed me?

PATIENCE [turning to him]
Fifteen years? What do you mean?

GROSVENOR
Have you forgotten the friend of your youth, your Archibald? — your little playfellow? Oh, Chronos, Chronos, this is too bad of you!

[Comes down, C.]

PATIENCE
Archibald! Is it possible? Why, let me look! It is! It is! [takes his hands.] It must be! Oh, how happy I am! I thought we should never meet again! And how you've grown!

GROSVENOR
Yes, Patience, I am much taller and much stouter than I was.

PATIENCE
And how you've improved!

GROSVENOR [dropping her hands and turning]
Yes, Patience, I am very beautiful! [Sighs.]

PATIENCE
But surely that doesn't make you unhappy?

GROSVENOR
Yes, Patience. Gifted as I am with a beauty which probably has not its rival on earth, I am, nevertheless, utterly and completely miserable.

PATIENCE
Oh — but why?

GROSVENOR
My child-love for you has never faded. Conceive, then, the horror of my situation when I tell you that it is my hideous destiny to be madly loved at first sight by every woman I come across!

PATIENCE

But why do you make yourself so picturesque? Why not disguise yourself, disfigure yourself, anything to escape this persecution?

GROSVENOR

No, Patience, that may not be. These gifts — irksome as they are — were given to me for the enjoyment and delectation of my fellow-creatures. I am a trustee for Beauty, and it is my duty to see that the conditions of my trust are faithfully discharged.

PATIENCE

And you, too, are a Poet?

GROSVENOR

Yes, I am the Apostle of Simplicity. I am called "Archibald the All-Right" — for I am infallible!

PATIENCE

And is it possible that you condescend to love such a girl as I?

GROSVENOR

Yes, Patience, is it not strange? I have loved you with a Florentine fourteenth-century frenzy for full fifteen years!

PATIENCE

Oh, marvelous! I have hitherto been deaf to the voice of love. I seem now to know what love is! It has been revealed to me — it is Archibald Grosvenor!

GROSVENOR

Yes, Patience, it is! [She goes into his arms.]

PATIENCE [as in a trance]

We will never, never part!

GROSVENOR

We will live and die together!

PATIENCE

I swear it!

GROSVENOR

We both swear it!

PATIENCE [recoiling from him]

But — oh, horror!

GROSVENOR

What's the matter?

PATIENCE

Why, you are perfection! A source of endless ecstasy to all who know you!

GROSVENOR
I know I am. Well?

PATIENCE
Then, bless my heart, there can be nothing unselfish in loving you!

GROSVENOR
Merciful powers! I never thought of that!

PATIENCE
To monopolize those features on which all women love to linger! It would be unpardonable!

GROSVENOR
Why, so it would! Oh, fatal perfection, again you interpose between me and my happiness!

PATIENCE
Oh, if you were but a thought less beautiful than you are!

GROSVENOR
Would that I were; but candour compels me to admit that I'm not!

PATIENCE
Our duty is clear; we must part, and for ever!

GROSVENOR
Oh, misery! And yet I cannot question the propriety of your decision. Farewell, Patience!

PATIENCE
Farewell, Archibald! [they both turn to go.]
[suddenly] But stay!

GROSVENOR
Yes, Patience?

PATIENCE
Although I may not love you — for you are perfection — there is nothing to prevent your loving me. I am plain, homely, unattractive!

GROSVENOR
Why, that's true!

PATIENCE
The love of such a man as you for such a girl as I must be unselfish!

GROSVENOR
Unselfishness itself!

No. 8a. Though to marry you would very selfish be
(Duet) Patience and Grosvenor

PATIENCE
Though to marry you would very selfish be—

GROSVENOR
Hey, but I'm doleful — willow willow waly!

PATIENCE
You may, all the same, continue loving me —

GROSVENOR
Hey willow waly O!

BOTH
All the world ignoring,
You'll/I'll go on adoring—
Hey, willow waly O!

[They go off sadly — PATIENCE, L., GROSVENOR, R.U.E.]

No. 9. Let the merry cymbals sound
(Finale of Act I) Ensemble

[Enter BUNTHORNE, crowned with roses and hung about with garlands, and looking very miserable. He is led by ANGELA and SAPHIR (each of whom holds an end of the rose-garland by which he is bound), and accompanied by procession of MAIDENS. They are dancing classically, and playing on cymbals, double pipes, and other archaic instruments. JANE last, with a very large pair of cymbals.]

[The procession enters over the drawbridge, BUNTHORNE being preceded by the CHORUS. They go R. and round the stage, ending with BUNTHORNE down L.C., with ANGELA on his R., SAPHIR on his L., JANE up C.]

MAIDENS
Let the merry cymbals sound,
Gaily pipe Pandaean pleasure,
With a Daphnephoric bound
Tread a gay but classic measure,
Tread a gay but classic measure.
Ev'ry heart with hope is beating,
For, at this exciting meeting
Fickle Fortune will decide
Who shall be our Bunthorne's bride!

Ev'ry heart with hope is beating,
For, at this exciting meeting

Fickle Fortune will decide
Who shall be our Bunthorne's bride!

Let the merry cymbals sound,
Gaily pipe Pandaean pleasure,
With a Daphnephoric bound
Tread a gay but classic, classic measure,
Tread a gay but classic, classic measure,
A classic measure.

[DRAGOONS enter down R., forming a line diagonally up to up-stage, C.]

CHORUS of DRAGOONS
Now tell us, we pray you,
Why thus they array you—
Oh, poet, how say you—
What is it you've done?

Now tell us, we pray you,
Why thus they array you—
Oh, poet, how say you—
What is it you've done?
Oh, poet, how say you—
What is it you've done?

DUKE [C.]
Of rite sacrificial,
By sentence judicial,
This seems the initial,
Then why don't you run?

COLONEL [R.C.]
They cannot have led you
To hang or behead you,
Nor may they all wed you,
Unfortunate one!

DRAGOONS
Then tell us, we pray you,
Why thus they array you—
Oh, poet, how say you—
What is it you've done?

[optional — Enter SOLICITOR.]

BUNTHORNE
Heart-broken at my Patience's barbarity,
By the advice of my solicitor

In aid — in aid of a deserving charity,
I've put myself up to be raffled for!

[He introduces his SOLICITOR]

MAIDENS
By the advice of his solicitor,
He's put himself up to be raffled for!

DRAGOONS
Oh, horror! urged by his solicitor,
He's put himself up to be raffled for!

MAIDENS
Oh, heaven's blessing on his solicitor!

DRAGOONS
A hideous curse on his solicitor!

MAIDENS
Oh, heaven's blessing on his solicitor!

DRAGOONS
A hideous curse on his solicitor!

MAIDENS	**DRAGOONS**
A blessing on his solicitor!	A curse, a curse on his solicitor!

[The SOLICITOR, horrified at the Dragoons' curse, rushes off, L.]

COLONEL [R.C. BUNTHORNE up L., surrounded by the LADIES]
Stay, we implore you,
Before our hopes are blighted;
You see before you
The men to whom you're plighted!

DRAGOONS
Stay, we implore you,
For we adore you;
To us you're plighted
To be united—
Stay, we implore you, we implore you!

DUKE [C.]
Your maiden hearts, ah, do not steel
To pity's eloquent appeal,
Such conduct British soldiers feel.
[Aside] Sigh, sigh, all sigh!

[They all sigh.]

To foeman's steel we rarely see
A British soldier bend the knee,
Yet, one and all, they kneel to ye—
[Aside] Kneel, kneel, all kneel!

[They all kneel.]

Our soldiers very seldom cry,
And yet — I need not tell you why—
A tear-drop dews each martial eye!
[Aside] Weep, weep, all weep!

[They all weep.]

MAIDENS & DRAGOONS
Our/We soldiers very seldom cry,
And yet — they/we need not tell us/you why—

ABOVE & DUKE
A tear-drop dews each eye/martial eye!
Weep, weep, all weep!

[The SOLICITOR re-enters]

BUNTHORNE [coming briskly forward, L.C.]
Come, walk up, and purchase with avidity,
Overcome your diffidence and natural timidity,
Tickets for the raffle should be purchased with avidity,
Put in half a guinea and a husband you may gain—
Such a judge of blue-and-white and other kinds of pottery—
From early Oriental down to modern terra-cottary—
Put in half a guinea — you may draw him in a lottery—
Such an opportunity may not occur again.

MAIDENS
Such a judge of blue-and-white and other kinds of pottery—
From early Oriental down to modern terra cottary—
Put in half a guinea — you may draw him in a lottery—
Such an opportunity may not occur again.

[MAIDENS crowd up to purchase tickets. DRAGOONS dance in single file round stage, to express their indifference.]

DRAGOONS
We've been thrown over, we're aware

But we don't care — but we don't care!
There's fish in the sea, no doubt of it,
As good as ever came out of it,
And some day we shall get our share,
So we don't care — so we don't care!

[During this the GIRLS have been buying tickets, the SOLICITOR officiating. At last JANE presents herself.
BUNTHORNE looks at her with aversion.]

BUNTHORNE
And are you going a ticket for to buy?

JANE [surprised]
Most certainly I am; why shouldn't I?

BUNTHORNE [aside]
Oh, Fortune, this is hard! [aloud]
Blindfold your eyes;
Two minutes will decide who wins the prize!

[GIRLS blindfold themselves.]

CHORUS of MAIDENS
Oh, Fortune, to my aching heart be kind;
Like us, thou art blindfolded, but not blind!
Just raise your bandage, thus, [Each uncovers one eye.] that you may see,
And give the prize, and give the prize to me! [They cover their eyes again.]

BUNTHORNE
Come, Lady Jane, I pray you draw the first!

JANE [joyfully]
He loves me best!

BUNTHORNE [aside]
I want to know the worst!

[JANE puts her hand in bag to draw ticket. PATIENCE enters and prevents her.]

PATIENCE
Hold! Stay your hand!

ALL [uncovering their eyes]
What means this interference?
Of this bold girl I pray you make a clearance!

JANE
Away with you, away with you, and to your milk-pails go!

BUNTHORNE [suddenly] She wants a ticket! Take a dozen!

PATIENCE
No! If there be pardon in your breast
For this poor penitent,
Who with remorseful thought opprest,
Sincerely doth repent;
If you, with one so lowly, still
Desire to be allied,
Then you may take me, if you will,
For I will be your bride!

[She kneels to BUNTHORNE]

CHORUS
Oh, shameless one!
Oh, bold-faced thing!
Away you run—
Go, take your wing,
Oh, shameless one!
Oh, bold-faced thing!
Away you run—
Go, take your wing,
You shameless one!
You bold-faced thing!

[BUNTHORNE raises her.]

BUNTHORNE
How strong is love! For many and many a week,
She's loved me fondly, and has feared to speak
But Nature, for restraint too mighty far,
Has burst the bonds of Art — and here we are!

PATIENCE
No, Mister Bunthorne, no — you're wrong again; Permit me — I'll endeavour to explain! True love must single-hearted be—

BUNTHORNE
Exactly so!

PATIENCE
From ev'ry selfish fancy free—

BUNTHORNE
Exactly so!

PATIENCE
No idle thought of gain or joy
A maiden's fancy should employ—
True love must be without alloy,
True love must be without alloy.

MEN
Exactly so!

PATIENCE
Imposture to contempt must lead—

COLONEL
Exactly so!

PATIENCE
Blind vanity's dissension's seed—

MAJOR
Exactly so!

PATIENCE
It follows, then, a maiden who
Devotes herself to loving you
Is prompted by no selfish view,
Is prompted by no selfish view!

MEN
Exactly so!

SAPHIR [coming L. of BUNTHORNE]
Are you resolved to wed this shameless one?

ANGELA [coming R. of BUNTHORNE]
Is there no chance for any other?

BUNTHORNE [decisively]
None!

[Embraces PATIENCE]

[Exit PATIENCE and BUNTHORNE, L. ANGELA, SAPHIR, and ELLA take COLONEL, DUKE, and MAJOR down, while GIRLS gaze fondly at other Officers.]

SEXTET
(ELLA, SAPHIR, ANGELA, DUKE, MAJOR, COLONEL)

I hear the soft note of the echoing voice
Of an old, old love, long dead—
It whispers my sorrowing heart "rejoice"—
For the last sad tear is shed—
The pain that is all but a pleasure will change
For the pleasure that's all but pain,
And never, oh never, this heart will range
From that old, old love again!

[GIRLS embrace OFFICERS]

CHORUS
Yes, the pain that is all but a pleasure will change
For the pleasure that's all but pain,
And never, oh never, our hearts will range
From that old, old love again!

DUKE	**CHORUS**
Oh, never, oh never	Oh, never, oh never
our hearts will range	our hearts, our hearts will range
From that old, old love again!	

SEXTET	**CHORUS**
Oh, never, oh never,	Oh, never, oh never our hearts,
our hearts will range	Oh, never, our hearts will range
From that old, old love again!	From that old, old love again!

[The GIRLS embrace the OFFICERS. Re-enter PATIENCE and BUNTHORNE. L.]

[As the DRAGOONS and GIRLS are embracing, enter GROSVENOR, R.U.E., reading. He takes no notice of them, but comes slowly down, still reading. The GIRLS are all strangely fascinated by him. The CHORUS divides, L. & R., and the GIRLS are held back by the DRAGOONS, as they attempt to throw themselves at GROSVENOR. Fury of BUNTHORNE, who recognizes a rival.]

ANGELA [R.C.]
But who is this, whose god-like grace
Proclaims he comes of noble race?
And who is this, whose manly face
Bears sorrow's interesting trace?

CHORUS
Yes, who is this, whose god-like grace
Proclaims he comes of noble race?

GROSVENOR [C.]
I am a broken-hearted troubadour,
Whose mind's aesthetic and whose tastes are pure!

ANGELA
Aesthetic! He is aesthetic!

GROSVENOR
Yes, yes — I am aesthetic
And poetic!

MAIDENS
Then, we love you!

[They break away from the DRAGOONS, and kneel to GROSVENOR.]

DRAGOONS
They love him! Horror!

BUNTHORNE and PATIENCE
They love him! Horror!

GROSVENOR
They love me! Horror! Horror! Horror!

ENSEMBLE
[all parts sung at the same time]

PATIENCE	**DUKE**
List, Reginald, while I confess	My jealousy I can't express,
A love that's all unselfishness,	Their love they openly confess;
That it's unselfish, goodness knows,	His shell-like ears he does not close
You won't dispute it, I suppose!	To their recital of their woes.

ELLA, SAPHIR, ANGELA, JANE	**CHORUS**
Oh, list while we a love confess	Oh, list while we/they a love confess
That words imperfectly express.	
Those shell-like ears, ah, do not close	That words imperfectly express.
To blighted love's distracting woes!	

ENSEMBLE
[all parts sung at the same time]

MAJOR, COLONEL & BUNTHORNE	**GROSVENOR**
My jealousy I can't express,	Again my cursed comeliness
Their love they openly confess!	Spreads hopeless anguish and distress,
Their love they openly confess, confess!	Spreads hopeless anguish and distress, distress!

MAIDENS	**DRAGOONS**
Yes, those shell-like ears, ah, do not close	Yes, his shell-like ears he does not close
To blighted love's distracting woes!	To their recital of their woes!

To blighted love's distracting woes,
their woes!

To their recital of their woes,
their woes!

ENSEMBLE
[all parts sung at the same time]

PATIENCE
Ah!
And I shall love you, I shall love.
Your ears, ah, do not close!
Thy shell-like ears, ah, do not close

To blighted love's distracting woes!

Thy shell-like ears, ah, do not close

To blighted love's distracting woes!

To love's, to love's distracting woes!
love's woes!

DUKE
Ah!
His shell-like ears he does not close
To love's distracting woes!
Now is not this ridiculous,
and is not this preposterous?
A thorough-paced absurdity,
explain it if you can!
Now is not this ridiculous,
and is not this preposterous?
A thorough-paced absurdity,
explain it if you can!
Explain, explain it if you can!
you can!

ELLA, SAPHIR, ANGELA, JANE
Oh, list while we our love confess
That words imperfectly express.
Thy shell-like ears, ah, do not close
To love's distracting woes!
Thy shell-like ears, ah, do not close
To blighted love's distracting woes!
Thy shell-like ears, ah, do not close
To blighted love's distracting woes!
To love's, to love's distracting woes!
Love's woes

MAIDENS
Oh, list while we a love confess
That words imperfectly express.
Those shell-like ears, ah, do not close
To love's distracting woes!
Those shell-like ears, ah, do not close
To blighted love's distracting woes!
Those shell-like ears, ah, do not close
To blighted love's distracting woes!
To love's, to love's distracting woes!
Love's woes!

BUNTHORNE
My jealousy I can't express,
Their love they openly confess.
His shell-like ears he does not close
To love's distracting woes!
His shell-like ears he does not close

To blighted love's distracting woes!

His shell-like ears he does not close

To blighted love's distracting woes!

To love's, to love's distracting woes!
Love's woes!

MAJOR and COLONEL
My jealousy I can't express,
Their love they openly confess.
His shell-like ears he does not close
To love's distracting woes!
Now is not this ridiculous,
and is not this preposterous?
A thorough-paced absurdity,
explain it if you can!
Now is not this ridiculous,
and is not this preposterous?
A thorough-paced absurdity,
explain it if you can!
Explain, explain it if you can!
You can!

GROSVENOR	MALE CHORUS
Again my cursed comeliness	Oh, list while they a love confess
Spreads hopeless anguish and distress	That words imperfectly express.
Thine ears, oh, Fortune, do not close	His shell-like ears He does not close
To love's distracting woes!	To love's distracting woes!
My shell-like ears I can not close	Now is not this ridiculous,
	and is not this preposterous?
To blighted love's distracting woes!	A thorough-paced absurdity,
	explain it if you can!
My shell-like ears I can not close	Now is not this ridiculous,
and is not this preposterous?	
To blighted love's distracting woes!	A thorough-paced absurdity,
	explain it if you can!
To love's, to love's distracting woes!	Explain, explain it if you can!
Love's woes!	You can!

[GROSVENOR makes a wild effort to escape up-stage; the GIRLS drag him back and kneel as the curtain falls.]

END OF ACT I

ACT II

[SCENE — A wooded glade, with a view of open country in the background. The chorus of MAIDENS is heard singing in the distance. JANE is discovered leaning on a violoncello, which she has propped up on a tree-stump, L., and upon which she will presently accompany herself. As the Chorus ends, she speaks.]

No. 10. On such eyes as maidens cherish
(Opening Chorus) Maidens

On such eyes as maidens cherish
Lest thy fond adorers gaze,
Or incontinently perish,
In their all-consuming rays!
Or incontinently perish,
In their all-consuming rays!

JANE
The fickle crew have deserted Reginald and sworn allegiance to his rival, and all, forsooth, because he has glanced with passing favour on a puling milkmaid! Fools! Of that fancy he will soon weary — and then, I, who alone am faithful to him, shall reap my reward. But do not dally too long, Reginald, for my charms are ripe, Reginald, and already they are decaying. Better secure me ere I have gone too far!

No. 11. Sad is that woman's lot

(Recitative and Solo) Jane

JANE
Sad is that woman's lot who, year by year,
Sees, one by one, her beauties disappear,
When Time, grown weary of her heart-drawn sighs,
Impatiently begins to dim her eyes!
Compelled, at last, in life's uncertain gloamings,
To wreathe her wrinkled brow with well-saved "combings,"
Reduced, with rouge, lip-shade, and pearly grey,
To "make up" for lost time as best she may!

Silvered is the raven hair,
Spreading is the parting straight,
Mottled the complexion fair,
Halting is the youthful gait,
Hollow is the laughter free,
Spectacled the limpid eye,
Little will be left of me
In the coming bye and bye!
Little will be left of me
In the coming bye and bye!

Fading is the taper waist,
Shapeless grows the shapely limb,
And although severely laced,
Spreading is the figure trim!

Stouter than I used to be,
Still more corpulent grow I—
There will be too much of me
In the coming by and bye!
There will be too much of me
In the coming by and bye!

[Exit, L., carrying her violoncello.]

[Enter GROSVENOR, R., followed by MAIDENS, two and two, playing on archaic instruments as in Act I.
He is reading abstractedly, as BUNTHORNE did in Act I, and pays no attention to them.]

No. 12. Turn, oh, turn in this direction
(Chorus) Maidens

Turn, oh, turn in this direction,
Shed, oh, shed a gentle smile,
With a glance of sad perfection,
Our poor fainting hearts beguile!

On such eyes as maidens cherish
Let thy fond adorers gaze,
Or incontinently perish,
In their all-consuming rays!
Or incontinently perish,
In their all-consuming rays!

[GROSVENOR sits, R.; they group themselves around him in a formation similar to that which opens Act I.]

GROSVENOR [aside, not looking up]
The old, old tale. How rapturously these maidens love me, and how hopelessly! [He looks up.] Oh, Patience, Patience, with the love of thee in my heart, what have I for these poor mad maidens but an unvalued pity? Alas, they will die of hopeless love for me, as I shall die of hopeless love for thee!

ANGELA
Sir, will it please you read to us?

GROSVENOR [sighing]
Yes, child, if you will. What shall I read?

ANGELA
One of your own poems.

GROSVENOR
One of my own poems? Better not, my child. They will not cure thee of thy love.

[All sigh.]

ELLA
Mr. Bunthorne used to read us a poem of his own every day.

SAPHIR
And, to do him justice, he read them extremely well.

GROSVENOR
Oh, did he so? Well, who am I that I should take upon myself to withhold my gifts from you? What am I but a trustee? Here is a decalet — a pure and simple thing, a very daisy — a babe might understand it. To appreciate it, it is not necessary to think of anything at all.

ANGELA
Let us think of nothing at all!

GROSVENOR [reciting]
Gentle Jane was as good as gold,
She always did as she was told;
She never spoke when her mouth was full,
Or caught bluebottles their legs to pull,

Or spilt plum jam on her nice new frock,
Or put white mice in the eight-day clock,
Or vivisected her last new doll,
Or fostered a passion for alcohol.
And when she grew up she was given in marriage
To a first-class earl who keeps his carriage!

GROSVENOR
I believe I am right in saying that there is not one word in that decalet which is calculated to bring the blush of shame to the cheek of modesty.

ANGELA
Not one; it is purity itself.

GROSVENOR
Here's another.

Teasing Tom was a very bad boy,
A great big squirt was his favourite toy
He put live shrimps in his father's boots,
And sewed up the sleeves of his Sunday suits;
He punched his poor little sisters' heads,
And cayenne-peppered their four-post beds;
He plastered their hair with cobbler's wax,
And dropped hot halfpennies down their backs.
The consequence was he was lost totally,
And married a girl in the corps de bally!

[The MAIDENS express intense horror.]

ANGELA
Marked you how grandly — how relentlessly — the damning catalogue of crime strode on, till Retribution, like a poised hawk, came swooping down upon the Wrong-Doer? Oh, it was terrible! [All shudder.]

ELLA
Oh, sir, you are indeed a true poet, for you touch our hearts, and they go out to you!

GROSVENOR [aside]
This is simply cloying. [aloud] Ladies, I am sorry to appear ungallant, but this is Saturday, and you have been following me about ever since Monday. I should like the usual half-holiday. I shall take it as a personal favour if you will kindly allow me to close early to-day.

SAPHIR
Oh, sir, do not send us from you!

GROSVENOR

Poor, poor girls! It is best to speak plainly. I know that I am loved by you, but I never can love you in return, for my heart is fixed elsewhere! Remember the fable of the Magnet and the Churn.

ANGELA [wildly]
But we don't know the fable of the Magnet and the Churn!

GROSVENOR
Don't you? Then I will sing it to you.

No. 13. A magnet hung in a hardware shop
(Solo and Chorus) Grosvenor and Maidens

GROSVENOR
A magnet hung in a hardware shop,
And all around was a loving crop
Of scissors and needles, nails and knives,
Offering love for all their lives;
But for iron the magnet felt no whim,
Though he charmed iron, it charmed not him;
From needles and nails and knives he'd turn,
For he'd set his love on a Silver Churn!

MAIDENS
A Silver Churn!

GROSVENOR
A Silver Churn!

His most aesthetic,
Very magnetic
Fancy took this turn—
"If I can wheedle
A knife or a needle,
Why not a Silver Churn?"

MAIDENS
His most aesthetic,
Very magnetic
Fancy took this turn—
"If I can wheedle
A knife or a needle,
Why not a Silver Churn?"

GROSVENOR [He rises, going C.]
And Iron and Steel expressed surprise,
The needles opened their well-drilled eyes,
The penknives felt "shut up", no doubt,
The scissors declared themselves "cut out",

The kettles they boiled with rage, 'tis said,
While ev'ry nail went off its head,
And hither and thither began to roam,
Till a hammer came up and drove them home.

MAIDENS
It drove them home?

GROSVENOR
It drove them home!

While this magnetic,
Peripatetic
Lover he lived to learn,
By no endeavour
Can magnet ever
Attract a Silver Churn!

MAIDENS
While this magnetic,
Peripatetic
Lover he lived to learn,

MAIDENS and GROSVENOR
By no endeavour
Can magnet ever
Attract a Silver Churn!

[They go off in low spirits, R.U.E., gazing back at him from time to time.]

GROSVENOR
At last they are gone! What is this mysterious fascination that I seem to exercise over all I come across? A curse on my fatal beauty, for I am sick of conquests!

[Goes R.]

[Enter PATIENCE, L. Stops L.C. on seeing GROSVENOR.]

GROSVENOR [Turns and sees her.]
Patience!

PATIENCE
I have escaped with difficulty from my Reginald. I wanted to see you so much that I might ask you if you still love me as fondly as ever?

GROSVENOR
Love you? If the devotion of a lifetime— [seizing her hand.]

PATIENCE [indignantly]

Hold! Unhand me, or I scream! [He releases her.] If you are a gentleman, pray remember that I am another's! [very tenderly.] But you do love me, don't you?

GROSVENOR

Madly, hopelessly, despairingly!

PATIENCE

That's right! I never can be yours; but that's right!

GROSVENOR

And you love this Bunthorne?

PATIENCE

With a heart-whole ecstasy that withers, and scorches, and burns, and stings! [sadly] It is my duty.

GROSVENOR

Admirable girl! But you are not happy with him?

PATIENCE

Happy? I am miserable beyond description!

GROSVENOR

That's right! I never can be yours; but that's right!

PATIENCE

But go now. I see dear Reginald approaching. Farewell, dear Archibald; I cannot tell you how happy it has made me to know that you still love me.

GROSVENOR

Ah, if I only dared— [advancing towards her]

PATIENCE

Sir! this language to one who is promised to another! [tenderly] Oh, Archibald, think of me sometimes, for my heart is breaking! He is unkind to me, and you would be so loving!

GROSVENOR

Loving! [advancing towards her]

PATIENCE

Advance one step, and as I am a good and pure woman, I scream! [tenderly] Farewell, Archibald! [sternly] Stop there! [tenderly] Think of me sometimes! [angrily] Advance at your peril! Once more, adieu!

[GROSVENOR sighs, gazes sorrowfully at her, sighs deeply, and exits, R. She bursts into tears.]

[Enter BUNTHORNE, followed by JANE. He is moody and preoccupied.]

In a doleful train
(Solo) Jane

JANE
In a doleful train
One and one I walk all day;
For I love in vain—
None so sorrowful as they
Who can only sigh and say,
Woe is me, alackaday!

BUNTHORNE [seeing PATIENCE]
Crying, eh? What are you crying about?

PATIENCE
I've only been thinking how dearly I love you!

BUNTHORNE
Love me! Bah!

JANE
Love him! Bah!

BUNTHORNE [to JANE]
Don't you interfere.

JANE
He always crushes me!

PATIENCE [going to him]
What is the matter, dear Reginald? If you have any sorrow, tell it to me, that I may share it with you.
[sighing] It is my duty!

BUNTHORNE [snappishly]
Whom were you talking with just now?

PATIENCE
With dear Archibald.

BUNTHORNE [furiously]
With dear Archibald! Upon my honour, this is too much!

JANE
A great deal too much!

BUNTHORNE [angrily to JANE]
Do be quiet!

JANE
Crushed again!

PATIENCE
I think he is the noblest, purest, and most perfect being I have ever met. But I don't love him. It is true that he is devotedly attached to me, but I don't love him. Whenever he grows affectionate, I scream. It is my duty! [sighing]

BUNTHORNE
I dare say!

JANE
So do I! I dare say!

PATIENCE
Why, how could I love him and love you too? You can't love two people at once!

BUNTHORNE
Oh, can't you, though!

PATIENCE
No, you can't; I only wish you could.

BUNTHORNE
I don't believe you know what love is!

PATIENCE [sighing]
Yes, I do. There was a happy time when I didn't, but a bitter experience has taught me.

[BUNTHORNE, noticing that JANE is not looking at him, goes off quickly up R. She turns, sees him, and runs after him.]

No. 14. Love is a plaintive song
(Solo) Patience

PATIENCE
Love is a plaintive song,
Sung by a suff'ring maid,
Telling a tale of wrong,
Telling of hope betrayed;
Tuned to each changing note,
Sorry when he is sad,
Blind to his ev'ry mote,
Merry when he is glad!
Merry when he is glad!
Love that no wrong can cure,
Love that is always new,
That is the love that's pure,

That is the love that's true!
Love that no wrong can cure,
Love that is always new,
That is the love that's pure,
That is the love, the love that's true!

Rendering good for ill,
Smiling at ev'ry frown,
Yielding your own self-will,
Laughing your teardrops down;
Never a selfish whim,
Trouble, or pain to stir;
Everything for him,
Nothing at all for her!
Nothing at all for her!
Love that will aye endure,
Though the rewards be few,
That is the love that's pure,
That is the love that's true!
Love that will aye endure,
Though the rewards be few,
That is the love that's pure,
That is the love, the love that's true!

[At the end of ballad exit PATIENCE, L., weeping. Enter BUNTHORNE, R., JANE following.]

BUNTHORNE
Everything has gone wrong with me since that smug-faced idiot came here. Before that I was admired — I may say, loved.

JANE
Too mild — adored!

BUNTHORNE
Do let a poet soliloquize! The damozels used to follow me wherever I went; now they all follow him!

JANE
Not all! I am still faithful to you.

BUNTHORNE
Yes, and a pretty damozel you are!

JANE
No, not pretty. Massive. Cheer up! I will never leave you, I swear it!

BUNTHORNE
Oh, thank you! I know what it is; it's his confounded mildness. They find me too highly spiced, if you please! And no doubt I am highly spiced.

JANE
Not for my taste!

BUNTHORNE [savagely]
No, but I am for theirs. But I will show the world I can be as mild as he. If they want insipidity, they
shall have it. I'll meet this fellow on his own ground and beat him on it.

JANE
You shall. And I will help you.

BUNTHORNE
You will? Jane, there's a good deal of good in you, after all!

No. 15. So go to him and say to him
(Duet) Jane and Bunthorne

[Dance]

JANE
So go to him and say to him, with compliment ironical—

BUNTHORNE
Sing "Hey to you—
Good-day to you"—
And that's what I shall say!

JANE
"Your style is much too sanctified — your cut is too canonical"—

BUNTHORNE
Sing "Bah to you—
Ha! ha! to you"—
And that's what I shall say!

JANE
"I was the beau ideal of the morbid young aesthetical—
To doubt my inspiration was regarded as heretical—
Until you cut me out with your placidity emetical."

BUNTHORNE
Sing "Booh to you—
Pooh, pooh to you"—
And that's what I shall say!
Sing "Booh to you—
Pooh, pooh to you"—
And that's what I shall say!

JANE

Sing "Hey to you — good-day to you"—
Sing "Bah to you — ha! ha! to you"—
Sing "Booh to you — pooh, pooh to you"—
And that's what you should say!

Sing "Hey to you — good-day to you"—
Sing "Bah to you —ha! ha! to you"—
Sing "Booh to you"—
And that's what you should say!
"Bah, bah,"
And that's what you should say!
"Booh, booh,"
And that's what you should say!

BUNTHORNE

"Hey,
Good-day
Bah.
ha! ha!

"Booh,
pooh-pooh
Bah.
And that's what I shall say!
"Booh, booh,"
And that's what I shall say!
"Bah, bah,"
And that's what I shall say!

BUNTHORNE

I'll tell him that unless he will consent to be more jocular—

JANE

Sing "Booh to you—
Pooh, pooh to you"—
And that's what you should say!

BUNTHORNE

To cut his curly hair, and stick an eyeglass in his ocular—

JANE

Sing "Bah to you—
Ha! ha! to you"—
And that's what you should say!

BUNTHORNE

To stuff his conversation full of quibble and of quiddity,
To dine on chops and roly-poly pudding with avidity—
He'd better clear away with all convenient rapidity.

JANE

Sing "Hey to you—
Good-day to you"—
And that's what you should say!

BUNTHORNE

Sing "Booh to you—
Pooh, pooh to you"—
And that's what I shall say!

JANE

Sing "Hey to you — good-day to you"—

BUNTHORNE

"Hey,

Sing "Bah to you — ha! ha! to you"—   Good-day
Sing "Booh to you — pooh, pooh to you"—   Bah.
And that's what you should say!   ha! ha!

Sing "Hey to you — good-day to you"—   "Booh,
Sing "Bah to you — ha! ha! to you"—   pooh-pooh
Sing "Booh to you"—   Bah.
And that's what you should say!   And that's what I shall say!
"Bah, bah,"   "Booh, booh,"
And that's what you should say!   And that's what I shall say!
"Booh, booh,"   "Bah, bah,"
And that's what you should say!   And that's what I shall say!

[They dance off, L.]

[Enter DUKE, COLONEL, and MAJOR, R. They have abandoned their uniforms, and are dressed and made up in imitation of Aesthetics. They have long hair, and other signs of attachment to the brotherhood. As they sing they walk in stiff, constrained, and angular attitudes—a grotesque exaggeration of the attitudes adopted by BUNTHORNE and the young LADIES in Act I.]

[Enter DUKE... enter MAJOR... enter COLONEL, Attitude. They walk to C.]

No. 16. It's clear that mediaeval art
(Trio) Duke, Major, and Colonel

ALL
It's clear that medieval art alone retains its zest,
To charm and please its devotees we've done our little best.
We're not quite sure if all we do has the Early English ring;
But, as far as we can judge, it's something like this sort of thing:
You hold yourself like this, [attitude]
You hold yourself like that, [attitude]
By hook and crook you try to look both angular and flat
[attitude].
We venture to expect
That what we recollect,
Though but a part of true High Art, will have its due effect.

If this is not exactly right, we hope you won't upbraid;
You can't get high Aesthetic tastes, like trousers, ready made.
True views on Medieavalism Time alone will bring,
But, as far as we can judge, it's something like this sort of thing:
You hold yourself like this, [attitude]
You hold yourself like that, [attitude]
By hook and crook you try to look both angular and flat
[attitude].
To cultivate the trim
Rigidity of limb,

You ought to get a Marionette, and form your style on him [attitude].

[Attitudes change in time to the music.]

COLONEL [attitude]
Yes, it's quite clear that our only chance of making a lasting impression on these young ladies is to become as aesthetic as they are.

MAJOR [attitude]
No doubt. The only question is how far we've succeeded in doing so. I don't know why, but I've an idea that this is not quite right.

DUKE [attitude]
I don't like it. I never did. I don't see what it means. I do it, but I don't like it.

COLONEL
My good friend, the question is not whether we like it, but whether they do. They understand these things — we don't. Now I shouldn't be surprised if this is effective enough — at a distance.

MAJOR
I can't help thinking we're a little stiff at it. It would be extremely awkward if we were to be "struck" so!

COLONEL
I don't think we shall be struck so. Perhaps we're a little awkward at first — but everything must have a beginning. Oh, here they come! 'Tention!

[They strike fresh attitudes, as ANGELA and SAPHIR enter, L.]

ANGELA [seeing them]
Oh, Saphir — see — see! The immortal fire has descended on them, and they are of the Inner Brotherhood — perceptively intense and consummately utter.

[The OFFICERS have some difficulty in maintaining their constrained attitudes.]

SAPHIR [in admiration]
How Botticelian! How Fra Angelican! Oh,
Art, we thank thee for this boon!

COLONEL [apologetically]
I'm afraid we're not quite right.

ANGELA
Not supremely, perhaps, but oh, so all — but! [to SAPHIR] Oh, Saphir, are they not quite too all — but?

SAPHIR
They are indeed jolly utter!

MAJOR [in agony]
I wonder what the Inner Brotherhood usually recommend for cramp?

COLONEL
Ladies, we will not deceive you. We are doing this at some personal inconvenience with a view of expressing the extremity of our devotion to you. We trust that it is not without its effect.

ANGELA
We will not deny that we are much moved by this proof of your attachment.

SAPHIR
Yes, your conversion to the principles of Aesthetic Art in its highest development has touched us deeply.

ANGELA
And if Mr. Bunthorne should remain obdurate—

SAPHIR
Which we have every reason to believe he will—

MAJOR [aside, in agony]
I wish they'd make haste! [The others hush him.]

ANGELA
We are not prepared to say that our yearning hearts will not go out to you.

COLONEL [as giving a word of command]
By sections of threes — Rapture! [All strike a fresh attitude, expressive of aesthetic rapture.]

SAPHIR
Oh, it's extremely good — for beginners it's admirable.

MAJOR
The only question is, who will take who?

COLONEL
Oh, the Duke chooses first, as a matter of course.

DUKE
Oh, I couldn't thank of it — you are really too good!

COLONEL
Nothing of the kind. You are a great matrimonial fish, and it's only fair that each of these ladies should have a chance of hooking you. It's perfectly simple. Observe, suppose you choose Angela, I take Saphir, Major takes nobody. [with increasing speed] Suppose you choose Saphir, Major tales Angela, I take nobody. Suppose you choose neither, I take Angela, Major takes Saphir. Clear as day!

[The OFFICERS, with obvious relief, abandon their aesthetic attitudes, and, with the LADIES, dance into position. L. to R. 1st verse: COLONEL with ANGELA; DUKE with SAPHIR; MAJOR alone. 2nd verse:

COLONEL alone; ANGELA with DUKE; SAPHIR with MAJOR. 3rd verse: COLONEL with SAPHIR; DUKE alone; ANGELA with MAJOR.]

No. 17. If Saphir I choose to marry
Quintet - Duke, Colonel, Major, Angela, and Saphir

DUKE
If Saphir I choose to marry,
I shall be fixed up for life;
Then the Colonel need not tarry,
Angela can be his wife.

MAJOR
In that case unprecedented,
Single I shall live and die—
I shall have to be contented
With their heartfelt sympathy!

ALL
He will have to be contented
With our/their heartfelt sympathy!
In that case unprecedented,
Single he/I will/shall live and die—
He/I will/shall have to be contented
With our/their heartfelt sympathy!
He/I will/shall have to be contented
With our/their heartfelt sympathy!
He/I will/shall have to be contented
With our/their heartfelt sympathy!

DUKE
If on Angy I determine,
At my wedding she'll appear,
Decked in diamond and ermine.
Major then can take Saphir!

COLONEL
In that case unprecedented,
Single I shall live and die—
I shall have to be contented
With their heartfelt sympathy!

ALL
He/I will/shall have to be contented
With our/their heartfelt sympathy!
In that case unprecedented,
Single he/I will/shall live and die—
He/I will/shall have to be contented

With our/their heartfelt sympathy!
He/I will/shall have to be contented
With our/their heartfelt sympathy!
He/I will/shall have to be contented
With our/their heartfelt sympathy!

[Positions at beginning of Verse 3: L. to R., COLONEL, ANGELA, DUKE, SAPHIR, MAJOR]

DUKE
After some debate internal,
If on neither I decide,
Saphir then can take the Colonel,

[Hands her to the COLONEL.]

Angy be the Major's bride!

[Hands her to the MAJOR.]

In that case unprecedented,
Single I shall live and die—
I shall have to be contented
With their heartfelt sympathy!

ALL
He will have to be contented
With our/their heartfelt sympathy!
In that case unprecedented,
Single he/I will/shall live and die—
He/I will/shall have to be contented
With our/their heartfelt sympathy!
He/I will/shall have to be contented
With our/their heartfelt sympathy!
He/I will/shall have to be contented
With our/their heartfelt sympathy!

[They dance off, arm-in-arm, up-stage and off, L.U.E., the COLONEL leading with SAPHIR.]

[Enter GROSVENOR, R.U.E.]

GROSVENOR
It is very pleasant to be alone. It is pleasant to be able to gaze at leisure upon those features which all others may gaze upon at their good will! [Looking at his reflection in hand-mirror.] Ah, I am a very Narcissus!

[Enter BUNTHORNE, L. moodily.]

BUNTHORNE

It's no use; I can't live without admiration. Since Grosvenor came here, insipidity has been at a premium. Ah, he is there!

GROSVENOR
Ah, Bunthorne! Come here — look! Very graceful, isn't it!

BUNTHORNE [taking hand-mirror]
Allow me; I haven't seen it. Yes, it is graceful.

GROSVENOR [taking back the mirror)
Oh, good gracious! not that — this—

BUNTHORNE
You don't mean that! Bah! I am in no mood for trifling.

GROSVENOR
And what is amiss?

BUNTHORNE
Ever since you came here, you have entirely monopolized the attentions of the young ladies. I don't like it, sir!

GROSVENOR
My dear sir, how can I help it? They are the plague of my life. My dear Mr. Bunthorne, with your personal disadvantages, you can have no idea of the inconvenience of being madly loved, at first sight, by every woman you meet.

BUNTHORNE
Sir, until you came here I was adored!

GROSVENOR
Exactly — until I came here. That's my grievance. I cut everybody out! I assure you, if you could only suggest some means whereby, consistently with my duty to society, I could escape these inconvenient attentions, you would earn my everlasting gratitude.

BUNTHORNE
I will do so at once. However popular it may be with the world at large, your personal appearance is highly objectionable to me.

GROSVENOR
It is? [shaking his hand] Oh, thank you! thank you! How can I express my gratitude?

BUNTHORNE
By making a complete change at once. Your conversation must henceforth be perfectly matter-of-fact. You must cut your hair, and have a back parting. In appearance and costume you must be absolutely commonplace.

GROSVENOR [decidedly]

No. Pardon me, that's impossible.

BUNTHORNE
Take care! When I am thwarted I am very terrible.

GROSVENOR
I can't help that. I am a man with a mission. And that mission must be fulfilled.

BUNTHORNE
I don't think you quite appreciate the consequences of thwarting me.

GROSVENOR
I don't care what they are.

BUNTHORNE
Suppose — I won't go so far as to say that I will do it — but suppose for one moment I were to curse you? [GROSVENOR quails.] Ah! Very well. Take care.

GROSVENOR
But surely you would never do that? [In great alarm]

BUNTHORNE
I don't know. It would be an extreme measure, no doubt. Still—

GROSVENOR [wildly]
But you would not do it — I am sure you would not.

[Throwing himself at BUNTHORNE's knees, and clinging to him]

Oh, reflect, reflect! You had a mother once.

BUNTHORNE
Never!

GROSVENOR
Then you had an aunt! [BUNTHORNE affected.] Ah! I see you had! By the memory of that aunt, I implore you to pause ere you resort to this last fearful expedient. Oh, Mr. Bunthorne, reflect, reflect! [Weeping]

BUNTHORNE [aside, after a struggle with himself]
I must not allow myself to be unmanned! [aloud] It is useless. Consent at once, or may a nephew's curse—

GROSVENOR
Hold! Are you absolutely resolved?

BUNTHORNE
Absolutely.

GROSVENOR
Will nothing shake you?

BUNTHORNE
Nothing. I am adamant.

GROSVENOR
Very good. [rising] Then I yield.

BUNTHORNE
Ha! You swear it?

GROSVENOR
I do, cheerfully. I have long wished for a reasonable pretext for such a change as you suggest. It has come at last. I do it on compulsion!

BUNTHORNE
Victory! I triumph!

No. 18. When I go out of door
(Duet) Bunthorne and Grosvenor

[Each one dances around the stage while the other is singing his solo verses.]

BUNTHORNE
When I go out of door,
Of damozels a score
(All sighing and burning,
And clinging and yearning)
Will follow me as before.

I shall, with cultured taste,
Distinguish gems from paste,
And "High diddle diddle"
Will rank as an idyll,
If I pronounce it chaste!

BOTH
A most intense young man,
A soulful-eyed young man,
An ultra-poetical, super-aesthetical,
Out-of-the-way young man!

GROSVENOR
Conceive me, if you can,
An ev'ryday young man:
A commonplace type,

With a stick and a pipe,
And a half-bred black-and-tan;
Who thinks suburban "hops"
More fun than "Monday Pops,"—
Who's fond of his dinner,
And doesn't get thinner
On bottled beer and chops.

BOTH

A commonplace young man,
A matter-of-fact young man—
A steady and stolidy, jolly Bank-holiday,
Every-day young man!

BUNTHORNE

A Japanese young man—
A blue-and-white young man—
Francesca di Rimini, miminy, piminy,
Je-ne-sais-quoi young man!

GROSVENOR

A Chancery lane young man—
A Somerset House young man,—
A very delectable, highly respectable
Three-penny-bus young man!

BUNTHORNE

A pallid and thin young man—
A haggard and lank young man,
A greenery-yallery, Grosvenor Gallery,
Foot-in-the-grave young man!

GROSVENOR

A Sewell and Cross young man,
A Howell & James young man,
A pushing young particle — "What's the next article?"—
Waterloo House young man!

BUNTHORNE	**GROSVENOR**
Conceive me, if you can,	Conceive me, if you can,
A crotchety, cracked young man,	A matter-of-fact young man,
An ultra-poetical, super-aesthetical,	An alphabetical, arithmetical,
Out-of-the way young man!	Every day young man!
Conceive me, if you can,	Conceive me, if you can,
A crotchety, cracked young man,	A matter-of-fact young man,
An ultra-poetical, super-aesthetical,	An alphabetical, arithmetical,
Out-of-the way young man!	Every day young man!

[GROSVENOR dances off, L.U.E.]

BUNTHORNE
It is all right! I have committed my last act of ill-nature, and henceforth I'm a changed character.

[Dances about stage, humming refrain of last air. Enter PATIENCE, L. She gazes in astonishment at him.]

PATIENCE
Reginald! Dancing! And — what in the world is the matter with you?

BUNTHORNE
Patience, I'm a changed man. Hitherto I've been gloomy, moody, fitful — uncertain in temper and selfish in disposition—

PATIENCE
You have, indeed! [sighing]

BUNTHORNE
All that is changed. I have reformed. I have modeled myself upon Mr. Grosvenor. Henceforth I am mildly cheerful. My conversation will blend amusement with instruction. I shall still be aesthetic; but my aestheticism will be of the most pastoral kind.

PATIENCE
Oh, Reginald! Is all this true?

BUNTHORNE
Quite true. Observe how amiable I am. [Assuming a fixed smile]

PATIENCE
But, Reginald, how long will this last?

BUNTHORNE
With occasional intervals for rest and refreshment, as long as I do.

PATIENCE
Oh, Reginald, I'm so happy! Oh, dear, dear Reginald, I cannot express the joy I feel at this change. It will no longer be a duty to love you, but a pleasure — a rapture — an ecstasy!

BUNTHORNE
My darling! [embracing her]

PATIENCE
But — oh, horror! [recoiling from him]

BUNTHORNE
What's the matter?

PATIENCE
Is it quite certain that you have absolutely reformed—that you are henceforth a perfect being — utterly free from defect of any kind?

BUNTHORNE
It is quite certain. I have sworn it.

PATIENCE
Then I never can be yours! [crossing to R.C.]

BUNTHORNE
Why not?

PATIENCE
Love, to be pure, must be absolutely unselfish, and there can be nothing unselfish in loving so perfect a being as you have now become!

BUNTHORNE
But, stop a bit. I don't want to change — I'll relapse — I'll be as I was — interrupted!

[Enter GROSVENOR, L.U.E., followed by all the young LADIES, who are followed by CHORUS of DRAGOONS. He has had his hair cut, and is dressed in an ordinary suit and a bowler hat. They all dance cheerfully round the stage in marked contrast to their former languor.]

No. 19. I'm a Waterloo House young man
(Solo and Chorus) Grosvenor and Maidens

GROSVENOR
I'm a Waterloo House young man,
A Sewell & Cross young man,
A steady and stolidy, jolly Bank-holiday,
Everyday young man.

MAIDENS
We're Swears & Wells young girls,
We're Madame Louise young girls,
We're prettily pattering, cheerily chattering,
Every-day young girls.

BUNTHORNE [C.]
Angela — Ella — Saphir — what — what does this mean?

ANGELA [R.]
It means that Archibald the All-Right cannot be all-wrong; and if the All-Right chooses to discard aestheticism, it proves that aestheticism ought to be discarded.

PATIENCE
Oh, Archibald! Archibald! I'm shocked — surprised — horrified!

GROSVENOR [L.C.]
I can't help it. I'm not a free agent. I do it on compulsion.

PATIENCE
This is terrible. Go! I shall never set eyes on you again. But — oh, joy!

GROSVENOR [L.C.]
What is the matter?

PATIENCE [R.C.]
Is it quite, quite certain that you will always be a commonplace young man?

GROSVENOR
Always — I've sworn it.

PATIENCE
Why, then, there's nothing to prevent my loving you with all the fervour at my command!

GROSVENOR
Why, that's true.

PATIENCE [crossing to him]
My Archibald!

GROSVENOR
My Patience! [They embrace.]

BUNTHORNE
Crushed again!

[Enter JANE, L.]

JANE [who is still aesthetic]
Cheer up! I am still here. I have never left you, and I never will!

BUNTHORNE
Thank you, Jane. After all, there is no denying it, you're a fine figure of a woman!

JANE
My Reginald!

BUNTHORNE
My Jane! [They embrace.]
Fanfare

[Enter, R., COLONEL, MAJOR, and DUKE. They are again in uniform.]

COLONEL
Ladies, the Duke has at length determined to select a bride!

[General excitement]

DUKE [R.]
I have a great gift to bestow. Approach, such of you as are truly lovely.

[All the MAIDENS come forward, bashfully, except JANE and PATIENCE.]

In personal appearance you have all that is necessary to make a woman happy. In common fairness, I think I ought to choose the only one among you who has the misfortune to be distinctly plain.

[GIRLS retire disappointed.]

Jane!

JANE [leaving BUNTHORNE's arms]
Duke!

[JANE and DUKE embrace. BUNTHORNE is utterly disgusted.]

BUNTHORNE
Crushed again!

No. 20. After much debate internal
(Finale of Act II) Ensemble

DUKE [R.C.]
After much debate internal,
I on Lady Jane decide,
Saphir now may take the Col'nel,
Angry be the Major's bride!

[SAPHIR pairs off with COLONEL, R., ANGELA with MAJOR, L.C., ELLA with SOLICITOR, L.]

BUNTHORNE [C.]
In that case unprecedented,
Single I must live and die—
I shall have to be contented
With a tulip or li-ly!

[BUNTHORNE, C., takes a lily from buttonhole and gazes affectionately at it.]

SAPHIR, ELLA, ANGELA, DUKE, BUNTHORNE and COLONEL
He will have to be contented
With a tulip or li-ly!

ALL
In that case unprecedented,
Single he/I must live and die—
He will/I shall have to be contented
With a tulip or li-ly!

Greatly pleased with one another,
To get married we/they decide.
Each of us/them will wed the other,
Nobody be Bunthorne's Bride!

Dance.

W.S. Gilbert – A Short Biography

Sir William Schwenck Gilbert was born on November 18th, 1836 at 17 Southampton Street, Strand, London. His father, also named William, was a naval surgeon, who later became a writer of novels and short stories, some of which were illustrated by his son. Gilbert's mother was the former Anne Mary Bye Morris (1812–1888), the daughter of Thomas Morris, an apothecary.

Gilbert's parents were distant and stern, and there was no close bond between either themselves or their children (the marriage was to eventually break up in 1876). Gilbert had three younger sisters, Jane Morris, Anne Maude Mary Florence.

As a child, Gilbert was nicknamed "Bab".

The family travelled to Italy in 1838 and then France before finally returning to settle in London in 1847.

Gilbert was educated in Boulogne, France from age seven, then at Western Grammar School, Brompton, London, before the Great Ealing School, where he became head boy and wrote plays for school performances. He then attended King's College London, graduating in 1856.

His first thought for a career was to take examinations for a commission in the Royal Artillery, but the Crimean War had just ended and with fewer recruits needed only a commission in a line regiment was available. He opted instead for the Civil Service and was an assistant clerk in the Privy Council Office for four years. He hated it. In 1859 he joined the Militia, a part-time volunteer force, and served until 1878, as his other work allowed, and reached the rank of Captain.

To supplement his income Gilbert wrote a variety of stories, comic rants, theatre reviews (many in the form of a parody of the play being reviewed), and, using the pseudonym of his childhood nickname, "Bab" illustrated poems for several comic magazines, primarily Fun, started in 1861. His work was also published in the Cornhill Magazine, London Society, Tinsley's Magazine and Temple Bar. Gilbert was also the London correspondent for L'Invalide Russe and a drama critic for the Illustrated London Times. In the 1860s he also contributed to Tom Hood's Christmas annuals, to Saturday Night, the Comic News and the Savage Club Papers.

The poems, illustrated humorously by Gilbert, proved immensely popular and were reprinted in book form as the Bab Ballads. He would later return to many of these as source material for his plays and comic operas.

In 1863 he received a bequest of £300 allowing him to leave the civil service and attempt a career as a barrister. Unfortunately, he managed to attract few clients.

However, these events happily coincided with his first professionally produced play; Uncle Baby, which ran for seven weeks in the autumn of 1863.

In 1865–66, Gilbert collaborated with Charles Millward on several pantomimes, including Hush-a-Bye, Baby, On the Tree Top, or, Harlequin Fortunia, King Frog of Frog Island, and the Magic Toys of Lowther Arcade (1866).

Gilbert's first solo success, however, came a few days after Hush-a-Bye Baby premiered. His friend and mentor, Tom Robertson, was asked to deliver a pantomime within two weeks. Robertson couldn't and recommended Gilbert who took the job. Written and rushed to the stage in 10 days, Dulcamara, or the Little Duck and the Great Quack, a burlesque of Gaetano Donizetti's L'elisir d'amore, proved very popular. This led to a long series of further Gilbert opera burlesques, pantomimes and farces, full of dreadful puns, but showing signs of the satire that would later be such an integral part of Gilbert's work.

After a failed relationship with the novelist Annie Thomas, Gilbert married Lucy Agnes Turner, whom he affectionately called "Kitty", in 1867; she was 11 years his junior. They were socially active both in London and later at their new home at Grim's Dyke, often holding dinner parties. Although they had no children they had many pets, including several exotic ones.

Next followed Gilbert's biggest success so far; his penultimate operatic parody, Robert the Devil, a burlesque of Giacomo Meyerbeer's opera, Robert le diable, part of a triple bill that opened the Gaiety Theatre, London in 1868. It ran for over 100 nights.

In Victorian theatre, Gilbert's burlesques were considered very tasteful compared to the offerings of others. He would now move away from burlesque to plays with original plots and fewer puns. His first was An Old Score in 1869.

Theatre, at this time had fallen into disrepute. London was awash with poorly translated French operettas and cheaply written, prurient Victorian burlesques. From 1869 to 1875, Gilbert joined with Thomas German Reed (and his wife Priscilla), whose Gallery of Illustration sought to regain some of theatre's lost respect with family entertainments. This would be so successful that by 1885 Gilbert could safely state that original British plays were appropriate for an innocent 15-year-old girl to watch.

The initial work for the Gallery of Illustration, No Cards, was the first of six musical entertainments for the German Reeds, by Gilbert some with music composed by Thomas German Reed.

The German Reeds' intimate theatre allowed Gilbert to develop a personal style that would also cede to him control all aspects of production; set, costumes, direction and stage management.

Gilbert's first big hit at the Gallery of Illustration, Ages Ago, also opened in 1869. It marked the beginning of a collaboration with the composer Frederic Clay that would last seven years and cover four works. It was at a rehearsal for Ages Ago that Clay introduced Gilbert to Arthur Sullivan.

These musical works gave Gilbert a valuable education as a lyricist and he perfected the 'topsy-turvy' style that he had been developing in his Bab Ballads, where the humour was derived by setting up a ridiculous premise and following through on its logical consequences, however absurd they might be.

Ever busy he found time to create several 'fairy comedies' at the Haymarket Theatre. The premise was the idea of self-revelation by characters under the influence of magic or some supernatural experience. The first was The Palace of Truth (1870), based partly on a story by Madame de Genlis. In 1871, with Pygmalion and Galatea, one of seven plays that he produced that year, Gilbert scored his greatest hit to date. Together, these plays including The Wicked World (1873), Sweethearts (1874), and Broken Hearts (1875), did for Gilbert on the dramatic stage what the German Reed entertainments had done for him on the musical stage: they established that his talents were large and burgeoning, a writer of wide range, as comfortable with human drama as much as farcical humour.

Contemptorous with this period Gilbert pushed the satirical boundaries. He collaborated with Gilbert Arthur à Beckett on The Happy Land (1873), in part, a parody of his own The Wicked World, which was briefly banned because of its caricatures of Gladstone and his ministers. Similarly, The Realm of Joy (1873) was set in the lobby of a theatre performing a scandalous play (implied to be the Happy Land), with many jokes at the expense of the Lord Chamberlain (the "Lord High Disinfectant", as he's referred to in the play). In Charity (1874), however, Gilbert uses the freedom of the stage in a different way: to illuminate the contrasting ways in which society treated men and women who had sex outside of marriage. It was ground breaking and some see it as anticipating the 'problem plays' of Shaw and Ibsen.

Once established as a writer Gilbert was also the stage director, with strong, forceful opinions on how they should best be performed.

In Gilbert's 1874 burlesque, Rosencrantz and Guildenstern, the character Hamlet, in his speech to the players, sums up Gilbert's theory of comic acting: "I hold that there is no such antick fellow as your bombastical hero who doth so earnestly spout forth his folly as to make his hearers believe that he is unconscious of all incongruity". Again some say with this he prepared the ground for playwrights such as George Bernard Shaw and Oscar Wilde to be able to flourish.

Tom Robertson had "introduced Gilbert both to the revolutionary notion of disciplined rehearsals and to mise-en-scène or unity of style in the whole presentation – direction, design, music, acting." Like Robertson, Gilbert demanded discipline in his actors, that they know their lines, enunciate them clearly and keep to his stage directions, a new development for actors at the time. It also ushered in the replacement of the star with the disciplined ensemble.

Gilbert was meticulous in his preparations, making models of the stage and designing every action in advance. He refused to work with actors who challenged him. He was famous for demonstrating the action himself, even as he grew older. Such was his interest in standards that even during long runs and revivals, he closely supervised the performances of his plays, making sure that no one made additions or deletions.

Sir Arthur Seymour Sullivan, MVO was born on May 13th 1842 in Lambeth, London. His father, Thomas Sullivan, a military bandmaster, clarinetist and music teacher, was born in Ireland and raised in Chelsea, London, and his mother, Mary Clementina (née Coghlan, English born, of Irish and Italian descent. Thomas Sullivan was based from 1845 to 1857 at the Royal Military College, Sandhurst, where he was the bandmaster and taught music privately to supplement his income. Young Sullivan became proficient with many of the instruments in the band and had composed an anthem, "By the waters of Babylon", by the age of eight. While proudly observing his son's obvious musical talent, he knew, at first hand, how insecure a profession it was and discouraged him from pursuing it.

Three years later whilst at a private school in Bayswater, Sullivan persuaded his parents and headmaster to allow him to apply for membership in the choir of the Chapel Royal. There were concerns that Sullivan at nearly 12 years of age was too old to be a treble as his voice would soon break. But he was accepted and soon became a soloist and, by 1856, was promoted to "first boy". Troublingly, even at this age, Sullivan's health was delicate, and he was easily fatigued.

However, Sullivan flourished under the training of the Reverend Thomas Helmore, and began to compose anthems and songs. Helmore arranged for one pieces, "O Israel", to be published in 1855.

In 1856, the Royal Academy of Music awarded the first Mendelssohn Scholarship to the 14-year-old Sullivan, granting him a year's training at the academy. His principal teacher there was John Goss, whose own teacher had been a pupil of Mozart. Initially Sullivan studied piano.

Sullivan's scholarship was extended to a second year, and then a third so that he could study in Germany, at the Leipzig Conservatoire. There he was trained in Mendelssohn's ideas and techniques as well as being exposed to Schubert, Verdi, Bach, and Wagner. Sullivan was an eager pupil and always looking for inspiration. On a visit to a synagogue, he was so struck by some of the cadences and progressions in the music that three decades later he would recall them for use in his serious opera, Ivanhoe.

Though the scholarship in Leipzig, was for one year he stayed for three. Sullivan credited his Leipzig period with rapid and sustained musical growth. His graduation piece, in 1861, was a set of incidental music to Shakespeare's The Tempest. Revised and expanded, it was performed at the Crystal Palace in 1862, a year after his return to London. It was an immediate sensation. He began building a reputation as England's most promising young composer.

He now embarked on composing with a series of ambitious works, interspersed with hymns, parlour songs and other light pieces of a more commercial nature. These compositions could not support him financially, and from 1861 to 1872 he supplemented his income working as a church organist, a task he enjoyed, and as a music teacher, sometimes at the Crystal Palace School, which he hated and gave up as soon as his finances allowed. Sullivan also took an early chance to compose pieces for royalty with the wedding of the Prince of Wales in 1863.

Sullivan began to put voice and orchestra together with The Masque at Kenilworth (Birmingham Festival, 1864). For Covent Garden that same year he composed his first ballet, L'île Enchantée.

1865 saw Sullivan initiated into Freemasonry and was Grand Organist of the United Grand Lodge of England in 1887 during Queen Victoria's Golden Jubilee.

In 1866, he premiered his Irish Symphony and Cello Concerto, his only works in these genres. In the same year, his Overture in C (In Memoriam), commemorating the recent death of his father, was a commission from the Norwich Festival.

His overture Marmion was premiered by the Philharmonic Society in 1867. The Times called it "another step in advance on the part of the only composer of any remarkable promise that just at present we can boast."

Sadly, his initial attempt at opera, The Sapphire Necklace (1863–64) with a libretto by Henry F. Chorley, was not produced and, apart from the Overture and two songs published separately, is now lost.

His first surviving opera, Cox and Box (1866), was written for a private performance. It then received charity performances in London and Manchester, and was later produced at the Gallery of Illustration, where it ran for an extraordinary 264 performances. His soon to be partner, W. S. Gilbert, writing in Fun magazine, announced the score as superior to F. C. Burnand's libretto.

In 1867 Sullivan and Burnand were commissioned by Thomas German Reed for a two-act opera, The Contrabandista (revised and expanded as The Chieftain in 1894), but it was a much more modest success.

Sullivan wrote a group of seven part songs in 1868, the best-known of which is "The Long Day Closes". His last major work of the 1860s was a short oratorio, The Prodigal Son, which premiered in Worcester Cathedral as part of the 1869 Three Choirs Festival to much praise.

The Overture di Ballo, Sullivan's most enduring work, was composed for the Birmingham Festival in 1870.

1871 was a busy year. Sullivan published his only song cycle, The Window; or, The Songs of the Wrens, to words by Tennyson, and wrote the first of a series of suites of incidental music for West End productions of Shakespeare plays. Later in the year he composed a dramatic cantata, On Shore and Sea, for the opening of the London International Exhibition, and the beautiful hymn Onward, Christian Soldiers, with words by Sabine Baring-Gould. The Salvation Army adopted it and it has become one of Britain's best loved hymns.

Gilbert & Sullivan – The Collaboration Begins

In 1871, John Hollingshead commissioned Gilbert to work with Sullivan on a holiday piece for Christmas, entitled Thespis, or The Gods Grown Old, at the Gaiety Theatre. It was a success and its run was extended beyond the length of the Gaiety's normal run. And that seemed to be that.

Gilbert and Sullivan now went their separate ways. Gilbert worked again with Clay on Happy Arcadia (1872), and with Alfred Cellier on Topsyturveydom (1874), as well as several farces, operetta libretti, extravaganzas, fairy comedies, adaptations from novels, translations from the French. In 1874, he published his last piece for Fun magazine ("Rosencrantz and Guildenstern"), almost three years after his last and then promptly resigned citing disapproval of the new owner's other publishing interests.

Sullivan was busy on large-scale works in the early 1870s with the Festival Te Deum (Crystal Palace, 1872); and the oratorio, The Light of the World (Birmingham Festival, 1873). He also wrote suites of incidental music for productions of The Merry Wives of Windsor at the Gaiety in 1874 and Henry VIII at the Theatre Royal, Manchester in 1877 as well as continuing composing hymns.

In 1873, Sullivan had also contributed songs to Burnand's Christmas "drawing room extravaganza", The Miller and His Man.

By 1875 conditions were right for Gilbert and Sullivan to work together again. Back in 1868, Gilbert had published a short comedic libretto in Fun magazine entitled "Trial by Jury: An Operetta". In 1873, Gilbert had arranged with theatrical manager and composer, Carl Rosa, to expand this work into a one-act libretto. It was arranged that Rosa's wife was to sing the role of the plaintiff. Tragically, Rosa's wife died in childbirth in 1874. Gilbert offered the libretto to Richard D'Oyly Carte, but Carte could not use the piece at that time.

The project seemed grounded. A few months later Carte, was managing the Royalty Theatre, needed a short piece to pair with Offenbach's La Périchole. Carte had previously conducted Sullivan's Cox and Box and remembering that Gilbert had suggested a libretto to him, he reunited Gilbert and Sullivan. The result was the one-act comic opera Trial by Jury. Starring Sullivan's brother Fred as the Learned Judge, it became a surprise hit, as well as earning lavish praise from the critics. It played for over 300 performances in its first few seasons.

A short time after Trial had opened Sullivan wrote The Zoo, another one-act comic opera, with a libretto by B. C. Stephenson. It did not perform well. Now the path was clear for Gilbert & Sullivan to reteam together in earnest and dominate light opera for the next 15 years.

Light opera was not considered of much worth by serious critics. Gilbert wanted greater respect for himself and his profession. At that time plays were not published in a form suitable for a "gentleman's library", they were in the main cheap and unattractive in their look designed mainly for use by actors rather than the home reader. Gilbert now arranged in late 1875 for the publishers Chatto and Windus to print a volume of his plays in a format designed to appeal to the general reader, with an attractive binding and clear type, containing Gilbert's most respectable plays, including his most serious works, and mischievously capped off with Trial by Jury.

After the success of Trial by Jury, there were discussions towards reviving Thespis, but Gilbert and Sullivan were not able to agree on terms with Carte and his backers. The score to Thespis was never published, and tragically most of the music is now lost.

Carte took some time to gather together funds for another opera, and in this gap the ever-busy Gilbert produced several works including Tom Cobb (1875), Eyes and No Eyes (1875), and Princess Toto (1876), his last and most ambitious work with Clay, a three-act comic opera with full orchestra. He also found time to write two serious works, Broken Hearts (1875) and Dan'l Druce, Blacksmith (1876) and his most successful comic play, Engaged (1877), which inspired Oscar Wilde's The Importance of Being Earnest.

It was only by 1877 that Carte finally assembled enough investors to form the Comedy Opera Company with a mandate to launch a series of original English comic operas, beginning with a third collaboration between Gilbert and Sullivan, The Sorcerer, in November 1877.

The Sorcerer (1877), ran for 178 performances, a success by the standards of the day, but H.M.S. Pinafore (1878), which followed it, turned Gilbert and Sullivan into an international phenomenon. The bright and cheerful music of Pinafore was composed during a time when Sullivan was in the middle of a health scare. He was in terrible pain from a kidney stone. H.M.S. Pinafore ran for 571 performances in London, the then-second-longest theatrical run in history, it also gave birth to and more than 150 unauthorised productions in America alone. Although this increased the reach of their reputations it added nothing to their profits.

It was noted in the Times review of H.M.S. Pinafore that the opera was an early attempt at the establishment of a "national musical stage" ... free from risqué French "improprieties" and without the "aid" of Italian and German musical models.

As the profits rolled in came acrimony among the investors who felt the shares were unequal. One night the other Comedy Opera Company partners hired thugs to storm the theatre to steal the sets and costumes in order that they could mount a rival production. This was beaten off by stagehands and others at the theatre loyal to Carte. Carte was to now continue as sole impresario of the newly renamed D'Oyly Carte Opera Company.

For the next decade, the Savoy Operas were Gilbert's principal activity. The successful comic operas with Sullivan continued to appear every year or two, several of them being among the longest-running productions of the musical stage. After Pinafore came The Pirates of Penzance (1879), Patience (1881), Iolanthe (1882), Princess Ida (1884 and based on Gilbert's earlier farce, The Princess), The Mikado (1885), Ruddigore (1887), The Yeomen of the Guard (1888), and The Gondoliers (1889). Gilbert not only directed and oversaw all aspects of production, but he designed the costumes himself for Patience, Iolanthe, Princess Ida, and Ruddigore. He insisted on precise and authentic sets and costumes, which provided a foundation to ground and focus his absurd characters and situations.

In 1878, Gilbert realised a lifelong dream to play Harlequin, which he did at the Gaiety Theatre in an amateur charity production of The Forty Thieves, written partly by himself. Gilbert trained for Harlequin's stylised dancing with his friend John D'Auban, who had arranged the dances for some of his plays and would choreograph most of the Gilbert and Sullivan operas. Producer John Hollingshead later remembered, "the gem of the performance was the grimly earnest and determined Harlequin of W. S. Gilbert. It gave me an idea of what Oliver Cromwell would have made of the character."

In 1879, Sullivan suggested to a reporter from The New York Times the secret of his success with Gilbert: "His ideas are as suggestive for music as they are quaint and laughable. His numbers ... always give me musical ideas."

During this time, Gilbert and Sullivan also collaborated on one other major work. In 1880, Sullivan was appointed director of the triennial Leeds Music Festival. For his first festival he was commissioned to write a sacred choral work. He chose Henry Hart Milman's 1822 dramatic poem based on the life and death of Saint Margaret the Virgin for its basis. It premiered at the Leeds music festival in October 1880. Gilbert arranged the original epic poem by Henry Hart Milman into a libretto suitable for the music.

Carte opened the next Gilbert and Sullivan piece, Patience, in April 1881 at London's Opera Comique, where their past three operas had played. In October, Patience transferred to the new, larger, state-of-the-art (it was the first theatre to be lit entirely with electricity) Savoy Theatre, built with the profits of the previous Gilbert and Sullivan works.

From now on all of the partnership's collaborations were produced at the Savoy. The first to actually premiere here was Iolanthe in 1882, it was their fourth hit in a row.

Cracks were beginning to surface between the partners. Sullivan, despite the financial security, began to view his work with Gilbert as beneath his skills, as well as being repetitious. After Iolanthe, Sullivan had not intended to write a new work with Gilbert, but when his broker went bankrupt in late 1882 he suffered serious financial loss. Needs must and Sullivan buckled down to continue writing Savoy operas. In February 1883, he and Gilbert signed a five-year agreement with Carte, requiring them to produce a new comic opera on six months' notice.

The ever watchful Gilbert had the previous year installed a telephone in his home and another at the prompt desk at the Savoy Theatre, so that he could listen in on performances and rehearsals from his home study. Gilbert had referred to the new technology in Pinafore in 1878, only two years after the device was invented and before London even had telephones.

Better news arrived for Sullivan on May 22nd, 1883, when he was knighted by Queen Victoria for his "services ... rendered to the promotion of the art of music" in Britain. The musical establishment, and many critics, believed that this would put an end to his career as a composer of comic opera – that a musical knight should not stoop below oratorio or grand opera. But Sullivan having just signed the five-year agreement and the financial security that gave him could no nothing to change course now.

The next opera, Princess Ida in 1884, which was the duo's only three-act, blank verse work, stuttered. Its run was much shorter. Sullivan's score was praised but with box office receipts lagging in March 1884, Carte gave the six months' notice, under the partnership contract, requiring a new opera.

Sullivan's friend, composer Frederic Clay, had suffered a serious stroke in early December 1883 that ended his career at only 45 years of age. Sullivan, with his own longstanding kidney problems, and his desire to devote himself to more serious music, replied to Carte, "It is impossible for me to do another piece of the character of those already written by Gilbert and myself."

Gilbert however was already at work on it. His idea revolved around a plot in which people fell in love against their wills after taking a magic lozenge. Sullivan was unequoviacal in his response. On April 1st, 1884 he wrote that he had "come to the end of my tether with the operas. I have been continually keeping down the music in order that not one syllable should be lost.... I should like to set a story of human interest & probability where the humorous words would come in a humorous not serious situation, & where, if the situation were a tender or dramatic one the words would be of similar character."

There was now a lengthy exchange of correspondence in which Sullivan called Gilbert's plot sketch (particularly the "lozenge" element) unacceptably mechanical, and too similar in both its grotesque "elements of topsyturveydom" and in actual plot to their earlier work, especially The Sorcerer, and requested, time and again, that a new subject be found.

This impasse was finally resolved on May 8th when Gilbert proposed a plot that would be their most successful: The Mikado (1885). It was to run for a staggering 672 performances.

In 1886, Sullivan composed his last large-scale choral work of the decade. It was a cantata for the Leeds Festival, The Golden Legend, based on Longfellow's poem of the same name. Apart from the comic operas, this proved to be Sullivan's best received full-length work. It was given hundreds of performances during his lifetime alone.

Ruddigore followed The Mikado in 1887. It was profitable, but its nine-month run was deemed to be disappointing compared with the earlier Savoy operas.

Gilbert was always keen to use a good idea again and proposed for their next piece another version of the magic lozenge plot. It was immediately rejected by Sullivan. Gilbert finally proposed a quite serious opera, to which Sullivan was in agreement. Although not a grand opera, The Yeomen of the Guard (1888) gave him the opportunity to compose his most ambitious stage work to date. In 1885, Sullivan had told an interviewer, ""The opera of the future is a compromise (among the French, German and Italian schools) – a sort of eclectic school, a selection of the merits of each one. I myself will make an attempt to produce a grand opera of this new school. ... Yes, it will be an historical work, and it is the dream of my life."

After The Yeomen of the Guard opened, Sullivan turned once again to Shakespeare and composed incidental music for Henry Irving's production of Macbeth (1888).

Sullivan wished to produce further serious works with Gilbert. He had collaborated with no other librettist since 1875. Gilbert felt the reaction to The Yeomen of the Guard had "not been so convincing as to warrant us in assuming that the public want something more earnest still." Gilbert countered by proposing that Sullivan should go ahead with his plan to write a grand opera, as well as comic works for the Savoy. Sullivan was not immediately persuaded. He replied, "I have lost the liking for writing comic opera, and entertain very grave doubts as to my power of doing it."

Nevertheless, Sullivan soon commissioned a grand opera libretto from Julian Sturgis (the recommendation came from Gilbert), while suggesting to Gilbert that he revive an old idea for an opera set in colourful Venice. The comic opera was completed first in 1889. The Gondoliers has been described as a pinnacle of Sullivan's achievement. It was to be the last great Gilbert and Sullivan success.

In April 1890, during the run of The Gondoliers, Gilbert objected to Carte's financial accounts which included a charge to the partnership for the cost of new carpeting for the Savoy Theatre lobby. Gilbert believed that this was a maintenance expense that should be charged to Carte alone. Carte who was building a new theatre to present Sullivan's forthcoming grand opera was adamant that it was legitimate. Sullivan sided with Carte, even going so far as to testify erroneously as to certain old debts.

The partners were in fundamental disagreement and the relationship was for all intents and purposes ruptured.

Gilbert took legal action against Carte and Sullivan and refused to write a word more for the Savoy. Sullivan wrote to Gilbert in September 1890 that he was "physically and mentally ill over this wretched business. I have not yet got over the shock of seeing our names coupled ... in hostile antagonism over a few miserable pounds".

From Gilbert's point of view Carte had either made a series of serious blunders in the accounts, or deliberately attempted to swindle his partners.

Gilbert wrote to Sullivan on May 28th, 1891, a year after the end of the "Quarrel", that Carte had admitted "an unintentional overcharge of nearly £1,000 in the electric lighting accounts alone." It seemed to illustrate Gilbert's point.

Work beckoned for Gilbert and he got on with it. He wrote The Mountebanks with Alfred Cellier and then a flop Haste to the Wedding with George Grossmith. Sullivan wrote Haddon Hall with Sydney Grundy.

In the Courts Gilbert prevailed in the lawsuit and felt vindicated. Although there was acrimony and bitterness between them the partnership had been so profitable that, after the financial failure of the Royal English Opera House, Carte and his wife sought to reunite the author and composer.

In 1891, after numerous failed attempts at a reconciliation, Tom Chappell, the music publisher who printed the Gilbert and Sullivan operas, stepped in to mediate between his two most profitable artists, and within two weeks, against the odds, had succeeded. The result was to be two more operas: Utopia, Limited (1893) and The Grand Duke (1896).

A third was almost achieved when Gilbert offered a third libretto to Sullivan (His Excellency, 1894), but his insistence on casting Nancy McIntosh, his protegée from Utopia, led to Sullivan's refusal.

Utopia, was only a modest success, and The Grand Duke, in which a theatrical troupe, by means of a "statutory duel" and a conspiracy, takes political control of a grand duchy, was a failure.

The partnership now ended for good.

Graciously Gilbert would late write, "... Savoy opera was snuffed out by the deplorable death of my distinguished collaborator, Sir Arthur Sullivan. When that event occurred, I saw no one with whom I felt that I could work with satisfaction and success, and so I discontinued to write libretti."

WS Gilbert – Life After the Partnership

In 1889 Gilbert financed the building of the Garrick Theatre. The following year the Gilberts moved to Grim's Dyke in Harrow. In 1891, Gilbert was appointed Justice of the Peace for Middlesex. After casting Nancy McIntosh in Utopia, Limited, he and Lady Gilbert developed an affection for her, and she eventually gained the status of an unofficially adopted daughter, moving to Grim's Dyke to live with them. She continued living there, even after Gilbert's death, until Lady Gilbert's death in 1936.

Although Gilbert announced a retirement from the theatre after the poor initial run of his last work with Sullivan, The Grand Duke (1896) and the poor reception of his 1897 play The Fortune Hunter, he produced at least three more plays over the last dozen years of his life, including an unsuccessful opera, Fallen Fairies (1909), with Edward German.

Gilbert, as we know was very keen on keeping his plays in the shape they were originally intended and continued to supervise the various revivals of his works by the D'Oyly Carte Opera Company, including its London Repertory seasons in 1906–09.

The last play he wrote, The Hooligan, produced just four months before his death, is a study of a young condemned thug in a prison cell. Gilbert shows sympathy for his protagonist, the son of a thief who, brought up among thieves, kills his girlfriend.

This grim, yet powerful piece, became one of Gilbert's most successful serious dramas, and it is easy to see why many thought he was developing a new style only for death to rob us of what would surely be a fascinating journey.

In these last years, Gilbert wrote children's book versions of H.M.S. Pinafore and The Mikado giving, in some cases, backstory that is not found in the librettos.

Official recognition for him came on July 15th, 1907 with his knighthood in recognition of his contributions to drama. Gilbert was the first British writer ever to receive a knighthood for his plays alone—earlier dramatist knights were knighted for political and other services.

On May 29th, 1911, Gilbert was about to give a swimming lesson to Winifred Isabel Emery and 17-year-old Ruby Preece in the lake of his home, Grim's Dyke, when Preece lost her footing and called for help. Gilbert dived in to save her but suffered a heart attack in the middle of the lake and died.

William Schwenck was cremated at Golders Green and his ashes buried at the Church of St. John the Evangelist, Stanmore. The inscription on Gilbert's memorial on the south wall of the Thames Embankment in London reads: "His Foe was Folly, and his Weapon Wit".

George Grossmith wrote to The Daily Telegraph that, although Gilbert had been described as an autocrat at rehearsals, "That was really only his manner when he was playing the part of stage director at rehearsals. As a matter of fact, he was a generous, kind true gentleman, and I use the word in the purest and original sense."

Gilbert's legacy, aside from building the Garrick Theatre are the canon of Savoy Operas and other works that are either still being performed or in print all these years later. He has made a lasting and defining influence on both the American and British musical theatre. The innovations in content and form of the works that he and Sullivan developed, and in Gilbert's theories of acting and stage direction, directly influenced the development of the modern musical throughout the 20th century. Gilbert's lyrics use punning, as well as complex internal and two and three-syllable rhyme schemes, and served as a model for such 20th century Broadway lyricists as P.G. Wodehouse, Cole Porter, Ira Gershwin, and Lorenz Hart.

Gilbert's influence on the English language has also been marked, with well-known phrases such as "A policeman's lot is not a happy one", "short, sharp shock", "What never? Well, hardly ever!", and "let the punishment fit the crime" arising from his pen.

Sullivan's only grand opera, Ivanhoe, based on Walter Scott's novel, opened at Carte's new Royal English Opera House on January 31st, 1891. Sullivan completed the score too late to meet Carte's planned production date, and costs had overrun to such an extent that Carte insisted on a contractual penalty of £3,000 for the delay. However, when it opened it ran 155 consecutive performances, a wonderful run for a serious opera, and garnered good reviews. Afterwards, Carte was unable to fill the new opera house with other productions, and, unfairly, Ivanhoe was blamed for the failure of the opera house.

Later in 1891, New York beckoned for Sullivan and his music for Tennyson's The Foresters, which ran at Daly's Theatre in New York in 1892, but failed in London the following year.

Sullivan returned to comic opera, but needed a new collaborator. His next piece was Haddon Hall in 1892, with a libretto by Sydney Grundy based somewhat loosely on the elopement of Dorothy Vernon with John Manners. Although still comic, the tone and style of the work was more serious and romantic than the operas with Gilbert. It nonetheless enjoyed a run of 204 performances, and earned critical praise.

In 1894 Sullivan teamed up again with F. C. Burnand for The Chieftain, a heavily-reworked version of their earlier two-act opera, The Contrabandista, alas it failed.

The following year Sullivan provided incidental music for the Lyceum, this time for J. Comyns Carr's King Arthur.

As we know Gilbert and Sullivan did reunite for The Grand Duke in 1896. But it failed and they never worked together again. This did not affect the constant revival of their earlier operas at the Savoy.

In May 1897, Sullivan's full-length ballet, Victoria and Merrie England, opened at the Alhambra Theatre in celebration of the Queen's Diamond Jubilee. The work's seven scenes celebrate English history and culture, with the Victorian period as the grand finale. It ran for six months which was a great achievement. Following this was The Beauty Stone in 1898, with a libretto by Arthur Wing Pinero and J. Comyns Carr. Based on mediaeval morality plays the opera was a critical failure and, on the whole, a commercial failure running for only seven weeks.

Success came in 1899, to benefit "the wives and children of soldiers and sailors" on active service in the Boer War, when Sullivan composed the music of a jingoistic song, "The Absent-Minded Beggar", to a text by Rudyard Kipling. It was a sensation and raised a staggering £250,000 from performances and the sale of sheet music and other merchandise. Later that year he returned to his comic roots with In The Rose of Persia, with a libretto by Basil Hood overlapping a setting of exotic Arabian Nights with plot elements of The Mikado. It was well received, and, apart from those with Gilbert, was his most successful full-length collaboration. Another opera with Hood, The Emerald Isle, quickly went into preparation, but sadly Sullivan died before it completion.

On November 22nd, 1900 Arthur Seymour Sullivan died of heart failure, following an attack of bronchitis, at his flat in London. The unfinished opera, The Emerald Isle, was completed by Edward German and premiered in 1901. His Te Deum Laudamus, written to commemorate the end of the Boer War, was performed posthumously.

Sullivan wished to be buried in Brompton Cemetery with his parents and brother, but by order of the Queen he was buried in St. Paul's Cathedral. In addition to his knighthood, honours awarded to Sullivan in his lifetime included Doctor in Music, honoris causa, by the universities of Cambridge (1876) and Oxford (1879); Chevalier, Légion d'honneur, France (1878); The Order of the Medjidieh conferred by the Sultan of Turkey (1888); and appointment as a Member of the Fourth Class of the Royal Victorian Order (MVO) in 1897.

In all, Sullivan's artistic output included 23 operas, 13 major orchestral works, eight choral works and oratorios, two ballets, one song cycle, incidental music to several plays, numerous hymns and other church pieces, and a large body of songs, parlour ballads, part songs, carols, and piano and chamber pieces.

Although Sullivan had several long term affairs and was also known to have a roving eye that led him to frequent liaisons with many other women he never married.

Rachel Scott Russell was the first of his great loves. Her parents' disapproval meant they met secretly but by 1868, Sullivan was enmeshed in a simultaneous and secret affair with Rachel's sister Louise. Both relationships had ceased by early 1869.

Sullivan's affair with the American socialite, Fanny Ronalds, a woman three years his senior, who had two children began when they met in Paris around 1867. The affair began in earnest soon after she moved to London in 1871. Despite his wandering ways she was a constant companion up to the time of Sullivan's death, but around 1889 or 1890, the sexual relationship seems to have ended.

In 1896, the 54-year-old Sullivan proposed marriage to 22-year-old Violet Beddington but she refused.

The favourite playgrounds for Sullivan were Paris and the south of France, with friends ranging from European royalty to Claude Debussy, and where the casinos enabled him to indulge his passion for gambling.

Sullivan enjoyed playing tennis although, according to George Grossmith, "I have seen some bad lawn-tennis players in my time, but I never saw anyone so bad as Arthur Sullivan".

He was devoted to his parents, particularly his mother, until her death in 1882. Henry Lytton wrote, "I believe there was never a more affectionate tie than that which existed between Sullivan and his mother, a very witty old lady, and one who took an exceptional pride in her son's accomplishments.

Sullivan once explained his method of working; "I don't use the piano in composition – that would limit me terribly". Sullivan explained that he did not wait for inspiration, but had "to dig for it. ... I decide on the rhythm before I come to the question of melody. ... I mark out the metre in dots and dashes, and not until I have quite settled on the rhythm do I proceed to actual notation."

In composing the Savoy operas, Sullivan wrote the vocal lines of the musical numbers first, and these were given to the actors. He, or an assistant, improvised a piano accompaniment at the early rehearsals; he wrote the orchestrations later, after he had seen what Gilbert's stage business would be. He left the overtures until last and often delegated their composition, based on his outlines, to his assistants, often adding his suggestions or corrections. Those Sullivan wrote himself include Thespis, Iolanthe, Princess Ida, The Yeomen of the Guard, The Gondoliers, The Grand Duke and probably Utopia Limited. Most of the overtures are structured as a potpourri of tunes from the operas in three sections: fast, slow and fast. The overtures from the Gilbert and Sullivan operas remain popular. Sullivan invariably conducted the operas on their opening nights.

In general, Sullivan preferred to write in major keys. In the Savoy operas less than 5% of the numbers are in a minor key and even in his serious works the major prevails. Sullivan was happy on occasion to use chords traditionally considered technically incorrect. When reproached for using consecutive fifths in Cox and Box, he replied "if 5ths turn up it doesn't matter, so long as there is no offence to the ear."

Sullivan's orchestra for the Savoy Operas was typical of any other pit orchestra of his era: 2 flutes (+ piccolo), oboe, 2 clarinets, bassoon, 2 horns, 2 cornets, 2 trombones, timpani, percussion and strings. According to Geoffrey Toye, the number of players in the Savoy orchestra was originally 31. Sullivan argued hard for an increase in the pit orchestra's size, and starting with The Yeomen of the Guard, the orchestra was augmented with a second bassoon and a bass trombone. Sullivan generally orchestrated each score at almost the last moment, noting that the accompaniment for an opera had to wait until he saw the staging, so that he could judge how heavily or lightly to orchestrate each part of the music. For his large-scale orchestral pieces, Sullivan added a second oboe part, sometimes double bassoon and bass clarinet, more horns, trumpets, tuba, and sometimes an organ and/or a harp. Many of these pieces used very large orchestras.

Sullivan's critical reputation has undergone extreme changes since he first came to prominence in the 1860s. At first, critics were struck by his potential, and he was hailed as the long-awaited great English composer. His incidental music to The Tempest received an acclaimed premiere at the Crystal Palace just before Sullivan's 20th birthday in April 1862. The Athenaeum wrote:

When Sullivan turned to comic opera with Gilbert, the serious critics began to express disapproval. Peter Gammond writes of "misapprehensions and prejudices, delivered to our door by the Victorian firm Musical Snobs Ltd. ... frivolity and high spirits were sincerely seen as elements that could not be exhibited by anyone who was to be admitted to the sanctified society of Art." As early as 1877 The Figaro wrote that Sullivan "has all the ability to make him a great composer, but he wilfully throws his opportunity away. ... He possesses all the natural ability to have given us an English opera, and, instead, he affords us a little more-or-less excellent fooling." Few critics denied the excellence of Sullivan's theatre scores. The Theatre wrote that "Iolanthe sustains Dr Sullivan's reputation as the most spontaneous, fertile, and scholarly composer of comic opera this country has ever produced." However, comic opera, no matter how skilfully crafted, was viewed as an intrinsically lower form of art than oratorio. The Athenaeum's review of The Martyr of Antioch declared: "It is an advantage to have the composer of H.M.S. Pinafore occupying himself with a worthier form of art."

Although the more solemn members of the musical establishment could not forgive Sullivan for writing music that was both comic and accessible, he was, nevertheless, "the nation's de facto composer laureate".

Gilbert & Sullivan – A Concise Bibliography

The Collaborative Pieces

All of these operas are full-length two-act works, except for Trial by Jury, which is in one act, and Princess Ida, which is three acts.

Thespis (1871)
Trial by Jury (1875)
The Sorcerer (1877)
H.M.S. Pinafore (1878)
The Pirates of Penzance (1879)
Patience (1881)
Iolanthe (1882)
Princess Ida (1884)
The Mikado (1885)
Ruddigore (1887)
The Yeomen of the Guard (1888)
The Gondoliers (1889)
Utopia, Limited (1893)
The Grand Duke (1896)

W.S. Gilbert – his Other Works

Poetry
The Bab Ballads, a collection of comic verse published roughly between 1865 and 1871
Songs of a Savoyard, London, 1890, a collection of Gilbert's song lyrics.

Short Stories
Foggerty's Fairy & Other Tales, a collection of short stories and essays, mainly from before 1874.

Some other short stories but not in the above appear here:-

Belgravia, Vol. 2 (1867). "From St. Paul's to Piccadilly," pp. 67–74
Fun, Vol. 1 new series (1865-1866) (several contributions by Gilbert; near end of volume)
Fun Christmas Number 1865, ("The Astounding Adventure of Wheeler J. Calamity,")
London Society, Vol. 13 (1868) (three "Thumbnail Sketches" by Gilbert)
On the Cards: Routledge's Christmas Annual (1867) ("Diamonds," and "The Converted Clown,")

Other Books
The Pinafore Picture Book, 1908, retelling the story of H.M.S. Pinafore for children, in prose narrative
The Story of The Mikado, 1921, a similar retelling of The Mikado for children

Plays and Musical Stage Works
Selected stage works that were important to Gilbert's career or were otherwise notable, in chronological order, excluding those listed under other headings below:

Dulcamara, or the Little Duck and the Great Quack (1866)
La Vivandière (1867)
Harlequin Cock Robin and Jenny Wren (1867), a Christmas pantomime.
The Merry Zingara (1868)
Robert the Devil (1868), it opened the Gaiety Theatre, London and ran in the provinces for 3 years.
The Pretty Druidess (1869), a parody of Norma – the last of Gilbert's five "operatic burlesques"
An Old Score (1869) (rewritten as "Quits!" in 1872) Gilbert's first full-length comedy.
The Princess (1870). Musical farce; the precursor to Princess Ida.
The Palace of Truth (1870).
Creatures of Impulse (1871), music by Alberto Randegger. From Gilberts story "A Strange Old Lady".
Pygmalion and Galatea (1871).
Randall's Thumb (1871). A comedy that opened the Royal Court Theatre.
The Wicked World (1873).
The Happy Land (1873). This work was briefly banned for its sharp satire of government ministers.
The Realm of Joy (1873).
The Wedding March (1873) a farce adapted from Un Chapeau de Paille d'Italie.
Rosencrantz & Guildenstern (published 1874, performed 1891). Gilbert's burlesque of Hamlet.
Charity (1874). Concerns Victorian attitudes towards sex outside of marriage.
Sweethearts (1874).
Tom Cobb (1875).
Broken Hearts (1875). The last of Gilbert's "fairy comedies", this was one of Gilbert's favourite plays.
Dan'l Druce, Blacksmith (1876).
Engaged (1877).
The Ne'er-do-Weel (1878); rewritten as "The Vagabond" after a few weeks.
The Forty Thieves (1878). Co-written with three other writers, WSG played Harlequin.
Gretchen (1879)
Foggerty's Fairy (1881)
Brantinghame Hall (1888) Gilbert's biggest flop, it sent producer Rutland Barrington into bankruptcy.
The Fortune Hunter (1897). Its reception provoked WSG to announce retiring from writing for the stage.
The Fairy's Dilemma (1904).
The Hooligan (1911).

German Reed Entertainments
Gilbert wrote six one-act musical entertainments for the German Reeds between 1869 and 1875. They were successful in their own right and also helped form Gilbert's mature style as a dramatist.

No Cards (1869)
Ages Ago (1869). Gilbert's first collaboration with Frederic Clay, ran for 350 performances.
Our Island Home (1870)
A Sensation Novel (1871)
Happy Arcadia (1872)
Eyes and No Eyes (1875)

Early Comic Operas
The Gentleman in Black (1870; music by Frederic Clay). The score is lost.
Les Brigands (1871), an English adaptation of Jacques Offenbach's operetta.

Topsyturveydom (1874; music by Alfred Cellier). The score is lost.
Princess Toto (1876; music by Frederic Clay). A three-act opera.

Though not as popular as the works with Arthur Sullivan, a few of Gilbert's later works arguably have stronger plots than the last two Gilbert and Sullivan operas.

The Mountebanks (1892; music; Alfred Cellier). This is the "lozenge plot" that Sullivan declined to set on several occasions.
Haste to the Wedding (1892; music; George Grossmith). An unsuccessful adaptation of The Wedding March.
His Excellency (1894; music; Osmond Carr). Gilbert felt that if Sullivan had set it, the piece would have been "another Mikado".
Fallen Fairies (1909; music by Edward German). Gilbert's last opera, which was a failure.

The Yarn of the Nancy Bell, with music by Alfred Plumpton. One of the Bab Ballads. 1869.
Thady O'Flynn, with music by James L. Molloy. 1868. From No Cards.
Would You Know that Maiden Fair, with music by Frederic Clay. From Ages Ago. c. 1869.
Corisande, with music by James L. Molloy. 1870.
Eily's Reason, with music by James L. Molloy. 1871.
Three songs from A Sensation Novel: "The Detective's Song", "The Tyrannical Bridegroom", and "The Jewel". 1871
The Distant Shore, with music by Arthur Sullivan. 1874.
The Love that Loves me Not, with music by Arthur Sullivan. 1875.
Sweethearts, with music by Arthur Sullivan. 1875.
Let Me Stay, with music by Walter Maynard. 1875.

The Sapphire Necklace (ca. 1863; unperformed)
Cox and Box (1866)
The Contrabandista (1867)
The Zoo (1875)
Ivanhoe (1891)
Haddon Hall (1892)
The Chieftain (1894)
The Beauty Stone (1898)
The Rose of Persia (1899)
The Emerald Isle (1901; completed by Edward German)

The Tempest (1861)
The Merchant of Venice (1871)
The Merry Wives of Windsor (1874)
Henry VIII (1877)
Macbeth (1888)
Tennyson's The Foresters (1892)
J. Comyns Carr's King Arthur for Henry Irving (1895)

Sheet Music

Ballets and Song Cycle
L'Île Enchantée (1864 ballet)
Victoria and Merrie England (1897 ballet)
The Window; or, The Song of the Wrens (1871 song cycle)

Choral Works with Orchestra
The Masque at Kenilworth (1864)
The Prodigal Son (Sullivan) (1869)
On Shore and Sea (1871)
Festival Te Deum (1872)
The Light of the World (Sullivan) (1873)
The Martyr of Antioch (1880)
Ode for the Opening of the Colonial and Indian Exhibition (1886)
The Golden Legend (1886)
Ode for the Laying of the Foundation Stone of The Imperial Institute (1887)
Te Deum Laudamus (1902; performed posthumously)

Orchestral Works
Overture in D (1858; now lost)
Overture The Feast of Roses (1860; now lost)
Procession March (1863)
Princess of Wales's March (1863)
Symphony in E, "Irish" (1866)
Overture in C, "In Memoriam" (1866)
Concerto for Cello and Orchestra (1866)
Overture Marmion (1867)
Overture di Ballo (1870)
Imperial March (1893)
The Absent-Minded Beggar March (1899)

Other Works

Songs & Parlour Ballads
Absent-minded Beggar (Rudyard Kipling) 1899

Arabian Love Song (Percy Bysshe Shelley) 1866
Ay de mi, My Bird (George Eliot)1874
Bid me at least Goodbye (Sydney Grundy) 1894
Birds in the Night (Lionel H. Lewin) 1869
Bride from the North (Henry F. Chorley) 1863
Care is all Fiddle-dee-dee (F. C. Burnand) 1874
Chorister, The (Fred. E. Weatherly) 1876
Christmas Bells at Sea (C. L. Kenney) 1875
County Guy (Walter Scott) 1867
Distant Shore, The (W. S. Gilbert) 1874
Dove Song (William Brough) 1869
E tu nol sai - see You Sleep (G. Mazzucato) 1889
Edward Gray (Alfred Tennyson)(1880
Ever (Mrs Bloomfield Moore) 1887
First Departure - see The Chorister (Rev. E. Munroe) 1874
Give (Adelaide Anne Procter) 1867
Golden Days (Lionel H. Lewin)1872
Guinevere! (Lionel H. Lewin) 1872
I Heard the Nightingale (Rev. C. H. Townsend) 1863
I Wish to Tune my Quiv'ring Lyre (Anacreon; trans. Lord Byron) 1868
I Would I were a King (Victor Hugo; trans. A. Cockburn) 1878
Ich möchte hinaus es jauchzen (A. Corrodi) 1859
If Doughty Deeds (Robert Graham of Gartmore) 1866
In the Summers Long Ago (J. P. Douglas) 1867
Let Me Dream Again (B. C. Stephenson) 1875
Lied, mit Thränen halbgeschrieben (Eichendorff)1861
Life that Lives for You (Lionel H. Lewin) 1870
Little Darling Sleep Again (Cradle Song) (anon) 1874
Living Poems (H. W. Longfellow)1874
Longing for Home (Jean Ingelow) 1904
Looking Back (Louisa Gray)1870
Looking Forward (Louisa Gray) 1873
Lost Chord, The (Adelaide Anne Procter) 1877
Love that Loves Me Not, The (W. S. Gilbert) 1875
Maiden's Story, The (Emma Embury) 1867
Marquis de Mincepie, The (F. C. Burnand) 1874
Mary Morison (Robert Burns) 1874
Moon in Silent Brightness, The (Bishop Reginald Heber) 1868
Mother's Dream, The (Rev. W. Barnes) 1868
My Dear and Only Love (Marquis of Montrose) 1874
My Dearest Heart (anon) 1874
My Heart is like a Silent Lute (Benjamin Disraeli) 1904
My Love - see "There Sits a Bird in Yonder Tree
My Love Beyond the Sea - see "In the Summers Long Ago"
None but I Can Say (Lionel H. Lewin)1872
O Fair Dove, O Fond Dove (Jean Ingelow) 1868
O Israel (Hosea) 1855
O Mistress Mine (William Shakespeare) 1866

O Swallow, Swallow (Alfred Tennyson) 1900
Oh Sweet and Fair (A. F. C. K.) 1868
Oh! bella mia - see "Oh! Ma Charmante"
Oh! Ma Charmante (Victor Hugo) 1872
Old Love Letters (S. K. Cowen) 1879
Once Again (Lionel H. Lewin) 1872
Orpheus with his Lute (William Shakespeare) 1866
River, The (anon) 1875
Roads Should Blossom, The (anon) 1864
Rosalind (William Shakespeare) 1866
Sad Memories (C. J. Rowe) 1869
Sailor's Grave, The (H. F. Lyte) 1872
St. Agnes' Eve (Alfred Tennyson) 1879
Shadow, A. (Adelaide Anne Procter)1886
She is not Fair to Outward View (Hartley Coleridge) 1866
Sigh no More, Ladies (William Shakespeare) 1866
Sleep My Love, Sleep (R. Whyte Melville) 1874
Snow Lies White, The (Jean Ingelow) 1868
Sometimes (Lady Lindsay of Balcarres) 1877
Sweet Day So Cool (George Herbert) 1864
Sweet Dreamer - see "Oh! Ma Charmante"
Sweethearts (W. S. Gilbert) 1875
Tears, Idle Tears (Alfred Tennyson) 1900
Tender and True (Dinah Maria Mulock) 1874
There Sits a Bird on Yonder TreeRev. (C. H. Barham) 1873
Thou art Lost to Me (anon) 1865
Thou art Weary (Adelaide Anne Procter) 1874
Thou'rt Passing Hence (Felicia Hemans) 1875
To One in Paradise (Edgar Allan Poe) 1904
Troubadour, The (Walter Scott) 1869
Village Chimes, The (C. J. Rowe) 1870
Weary Lot is Thine, Fair Maid, A (Walter Scott) 1866
We've Ploughed our Land (anon)1875
When Thou Art Near (W. J. Stewart) 1877
White Plume, The - see "The Bride from the North"
Will He Come? (Adelaide A. Procter) 1865
Willow Song, The (William Shakespeare)1866
You Sleep (B. C. Stephenson) 1889

Hymns (Title & First Line)
Adoro Te - Saviour, again to Thy dear name we raise (Arranger)
All This Night - All this night bright angels sing
Angel Voices - Angel voices, ever singing
Audite Audientes me - I heard the voice of Jesus say
Bethlehem - While shepherd's watched their flocks (Arranger)
Bishopgarth - O King of Kings, Whose reign of old
Bolwell - Thou to whom the sick and dying

Carrow - My God, I thank Thee Who has made
Chapel Royal - O love that wilt not let me go
Christus - Show me not only Jesus dying
Clarence - Winter reigneth o'er the land
Coena Domini - Draw nigh, and take the body of the Lord
Come Unto Me - Come unto Me, ye weary (Arranger)
Constance - I've found a Friend; oh, such a Friend
Coronae - Crown Him, with many crowns
Courage, Brother - Courage, brother, do not stumble
Dominion Hymn - God bless our wide dominion
Dulce Sonans - Angel voices, ever singing
Ecclesia - The church has waited long
Ellers - Saviour, again to Thy dear name we raise (Arranger)
Evelyn - In the hour of my distress
Ever Faithful - Let us with a gladsome mind
Fatherland (St. Edmund) - I'm but a stranger here
Formosa (Falfield) - Love Divine, all love excelling
Fortunatus - Welcome, happy morning!
Golden Sheaves - To Thee, O Lord, our hearts we raise
Hanford - Jesu, my Saviour, look on me
Heber (Gennesareth) - When through the torn sail
Holy City - Sing Alleluia forth in duteous praise
Hushed was the Evening Hymn - Hushed was the evening hymn
Hymn of the Homeland - The homeland, the homeland
Lacrymae - Lord, in this Thy mercy's day
Leominster - A few more years shall roll (Arranger)
Light - Holy Spirit! Come in might! (Arranger)
Litany (1) - Jesu, life of those who die
Litany (2) - Jesu, we are far away
Long Home, The - Tender Shepherd, Thou hast still'd
Lux eoi - All is bright and cheeful round us
Lux in Tenebris - Lead, kindly Light
Lux Mundi - O Jesu, Thou art standing
Marlborough - O Strength and Stay, upholding all creation (Arranger)
Mount Zion - Rock of Ages, cleft for me
Nearer Home - For ever with the Lord (Arranger)
Noel - It came upon the midnight clear (Arranger)
Old 137th - Great King of nations, hear our prayer (Arranger)
Paradise - O Paradise!
Parting - With the sweet word of peace (Arranger)
Pilgrimage - From Egypt's bondage come
Promissio Patris - Our blest Redeemer, ere He breathed
Propior Deo - Nearer, my God, to Thee
Rest - Art thou weary, art thou languid
Resurrexit - Christ is risen!
Roseate Hues, The - The roseate hues of early dawn
Safe Home - Safe home, safe home in port
St. Ann - The Son of God goes forth to war (Arranger)

St. Francis - O Father, who hast created all
St. Gertrude - Onward, Christian soldiers
St. Kevin - Come, ye faithful, raise the strain
St. Lucian - Of Thy love some gracious token
St. Luke (St. Nathaniel) - God moves in a mysterious way
St. Mary Magdalene - Saviour, when in dust to Thee
St. Millicent - Let no tears to-day be shed
St. Patrick - He is gone - a cloud of light
St. Theresa - Brightly gleams our banner
Saints of God - The Saints of God, their conflict past.
Springtime - For all Thy love and goodness (Arranger)
Strain Upraise, The - The Strain upraise in joy and praise
Thou God of Love - Thou God of Love, beneath Thy sheltering wing
Ultor Omnipotens - God the all terrible! King who ordainest
Valete - Sweet Saviour, bless us 'ere we go
Veni, Creator - Come Holy Ghost, our souls inspire
Victoria - To mourn our dead we gather here

Part Songs

The term "Part Song" is more usually applied to one where the highest part carries the melody with the other voices supplying the accompanying harmonies.

Also included here are the soprano duet, The Sisters, and the trio Sullivan composed for the play Olivia by W. G. Wills, Morn, Happy Morn.

O Lady Dear (Madrigal) - Composed 1857, unpublished.
It was a Lover and his Lass - Words by Shakespeare. Performed at the Royal Academy of Music, 1857, unpublished.
Seaside Thoughts - Words by Bernard Bartram. Composed 1857. Published 1904.
The Last Night of the Year - Words by H. F. Chorley. Published 1863.
O Hush Thee, My Babie - Words by Walter Scott. Published 1867.
The Rainy Day - Words by H. W. Longfellow. Published 1867.
Evening - Words by Lord Houghton, after Goethe. Published 1868.
Parting Gleams - Words by Aubrey de Vere. Published 1868.
Echoes - Words by Thomas Moore. Published 1868.
The Long Day Closes - Words by H. F. Chorley. Published 1868.
Joy to the Victors - Words by Walter Scott. Published 1868
The Beleaguered - Words by H. F. Chorley. Published 1868.
It Came Upon the Midnight Clear - Words by E. H. Sears. Published 1871.
Lead, Kindly Light - Words by J. H. Newman. Published 1871.
Through Sorrows Path - Words by H. Kirke White. Published 1871.
Say, Watchman, What of the Night? - Words from Isaiah. Published 1871.
The Way is Long and Dreary - Words by Adelaide Anne Procter. Published 1871.
Morn, Happy Morn - Composed for the play, Olivia by W. G. Wills. Published 1878.
The Sisters - Words by Alfred Tennyson. Published 1881.
Wreaths for our Graves - Words by L. F. Massey. Published 1898.

Fair Daffodils - Words by Robert Herrick. Published 1904.

By the Waters of Babylon - Composed c. 1850. Unpublished.
Sing unto the Lord - Composed 1855. Unpublished.
Psalm 103 - Composed 1856. Unpublished.
We have heard with our ears
(i) Dedicated to Sir George Smart and performed at the Chapel Royal, January 1860.
(ii) Dedicated to Rev. Thomas Helmore. 1865.
O Love the Lord - Dedicated to John Goss. 1864.
Te Deum, Jubilate, Kyrie (in D major) 1866.
O God, Thou art Worthy - Composed for the wedding of Adrian Hope, 3 June 1867. Published in 1871.
O Taste and See - Dedicated to Rev. C. H. Haweis. 1867.
Rejoice in the Lord - Composed for the wedding of Rev. R. Brown-Borthwick, 16 April 1868.
Sing, O Heavens - Dedicated to Rev. F. C. Byng. 1869.
I Will Worship - Dedicated to Rev. F. Gore Ouseley. 1871.
Two Choruses adapted from Russian Church Music, 1874.
(i) Turn Thee Again
(ii) Mercy and Truth
I Will Mention Thy Loving-kindness - Dedicated to John Stainer. 1875.
I Will Sing of Thy Power. 1877.
Hearken Unto Me, My People. 1877.
Turn Thy Face. 1878.
Who is Like unto Thee - Dedicated to Walter Parratt. 1883.
I Will Lay Me Down in Peace - Composed 1868. Published only in 1910.

Hearken unto me, my people - An Anthem for Advent or General Use. Words from Isaiah. (1877)

All this night bright angels sing - Words by W. Austin. (1870)
I Sing the Birth - Words by Ben Jonson. (1868)
It Came Upon the Midnight Clear - Words by E. H. Sears.
Part Song for Soprano Solo and Choir (1871)
Hymn Tune "Noel" (1874)
Upon the Snow-clad Earth (1876)
While Shepherds Watched - Words by Nahum Tate (1874)
Hark! What Mean those Holy Voices? - Words by John Cawood (1883)

Christmas Bells at Sea - Words by Charles Kenney (1875)

Two songs from The Miller and His Man - A Christmas Drawing Room Entertainment. Words by F. C. Burnand (1874)
The Marquis de Mincepie
Care is all Fiddle-dee-dee
The Last Night of the Year - Part Song - Words by H. F. Chorley (1863)

Chamber Music & Solo Piano
Scherzo - Piano Solo, 1857, unpublished.
Capriccio No. 2 - Piano Solo (unfinished), 1857, unpublished.
String Quartet - Performed at Leipzig, May 1859. Published 2000
Romance in G minor - For string quartet, 1859. Published 1964.
Thoughts - Two pieces for piano solo, Published by Cramer, 1862.
An Idyll - For Cello and Piano. Composed in 1865 and Published 1899.
Allegro Risoluto - Piano solo, 1866. Published only in 1974
Berceuse - Based on the theme of Hushed was the Bacon from Cox and Box but with additional material.
Day Dreams - Six pieces for piano solo. 1867
Duo Concertante - Cello and piano. 1868
Twilight - Piano solo. 1868

www.ingramcontent.com/pod-product-compliance
Lightning Source LLC
Chambersburg PA
CBHW060139050426
42448CB00010B/2204